PYTHON FOR EXCEL: PYTHON POWERED FORMULA ONE RACING

Hayden Van Der Post

Reactive Publishing

To my daughter, may she know anything is possible.

CONTENTS

Title Page

Dedication

Chapter 1: Introduction to Python and Excel Integration   1

Chapter 2: Foundations of Python Programming for   18
Excel Users

Chapter 3: Data Manipulation and Cleaning with Python   38
and Excel

Chapter 4: Advanced Excel Functions and Macros with   54
Python

Chapter 5: Statistical Analysis and Financial Modeling   71
with Python and Excel

Chapter 6: Integrating Python Machine Learning with   85
Excel

Chapter 7: Advanced Visualizations and Reporting with   103
Python and Excel

Chapter 8: Optimizing Performance and Efficiency in   126
Excel with Python

Chapter 9: Web Scraping and API Integration with   151
Python and Excel

Chapter 10: Building Custom Python Tools for Excel   173

Chapter 11: Case Studies and Real-world Applications   198

Chapter 12: Best Practices for Efficient Integration   224

Chapter 13: Security and Compliance 246

Chapter 14: Future Trends and Emerging Technologies 268

Chapter 15: Conclusion and Final Thoughts 289

CHAPTER 1: INTRODUCTION TO PYTHON AND EXCEL INTEGRATION

Why Python? Understanding its Benefits and Advantages over Excel

In the world of data analysis and automation, an intriguing question perpetually arises amongst the members of the financial industry - "Why choose Python?" Let's embark on an enlightening voyage through the realm of Python and its astounding capabilities.

Best known for its readability and simplicity, Python has seen a phenomenal rise in popularity, especially in the world of finance and data analytics. It distinguishes itself with an uncomplicated syntax that allows for easier readability and efficiency in coding. Its syntactical clarity leads to less time and effort being spent in writing and debugging, making it more cost-effective. In comparison, Excel, though widely accepted and used, may lack this level of intuitive operation.

The dichotomy between Python and Excel lies in their inherent natures — Excel, a spreadsheet tool, compared to

Python, a full-fledged programming language. Excel's strength lies in its grid-like interface, easy sorting and filtering of data, and as a repository for financial models. However, it lacks the fluid data manipulation, complex computations, and automation abilities that Python brings to the table.

One of the primary advantages Python holds over Excel is its capability to handle an immense amount of data. As datasets grow larger and more complex, the efficiency of Excel starts to dwindle. On the contrary, Python can perform complex data analysis and manipulations on huge datasets with ease, thanks to libraries like Pandas, NumPy, or SciPy.

Python's ability to integrate and communicate with other languages, APIs, and systems outshines Excel. By leveraging the powerful API interfaces provided by Python packages, you can integrate your financial models with live feeds of market data, social media sentiment, weather data, and more.

Python also breathes life into financial models. Unlike Excel models that are static, Python is capable of creating dynamic models. With Python's advanced libraries like TensorFlow, Keras, or Scikit-Learn, you can design sophisticated machine learning models for predicting future stock prices, evaluate portfolio risk, or detect fraudulent transactions.

Python, with its powerful and varied visualization libraries like Matplotlib, Seaborn, or Plotly, gives users an edge in creating more vibrant and dynamic visualizations. Excel's visualization features may suffice for standard bar, column, or pie charts but fall short when it comes to advanced graphical representations.

The supremacy of Python over Excel is realized once we

venture into the domain of complex data manipulation, sophisticated computations, and advanced modeling. Python's adaptive nature, with its far-reaching benefits in dealing with large datasets, automation, integration, and visualization, gears finance professionals towards a more efficient and robust approach. As an analyst or a developer, comprehending these strengths of Python sets the stage for leveraging the Python-Excel integration more effectively.

Remember, in the fast-paced technological era, Python isn't out to replace Excel but rather to complement and enhance it. By understanding when to use Python and when to stick to Excel, you can tap into the full potential of both, creating a synergy that will propel your financial analysis to new heights. And with that, let's delve further into the world of Excel's might.

The Power of Excel

Immersing ourselves further into this enlightening exploration, we find juxtaposition with Excel, a powerful tool, widely accepted in businesses all around the world. While Python brings along finesse and precision, let's take a moment to revisit the magnificent arena of Excel and its uncontested capabilities.

Microsoft Excel, a spreadsheet software, is a ubiquitous tool found in practically every business setting. Its primary capabilities involve storing, organising and processing data efficiently in an easy-to-read, grid-like format. But why does Excel stand proudly in the world of modern, fast-paced business technology and data analytics? What is it about Excel that makes it such a resilient and popular choice?

Excel's user-friendly interface is its foremost advantage. Designed for optimum ease of use, the grid of rows and columns makes data visualisation instinctive. Even with minimal technological expertise, an individual can organise and calculate data.

The embedded functions within Excel offer a host of arithmetic capabilities — from simple addition and subtraction to complex statistical analysis. These functions expedite the process of calculations and data analysis, eliminating potential errors.

A vital attribute of Excel is its pivot table functionality. It allows rapid summarisation of large data sets, unraveling crucial patterns and trends that would otherwise go unnoticed. Where Python requires lines of coding to perform the same operation, Excel provides a user-friendly, drag and drop interface.

What sets Excel apart is its capacity for 'What-If Analysis'. This function allows the prediction of outcomes based on a given set of variables, which is an indispensable tool in risk assessment and decision-making processes within the financial sector.

Moreover, Excel has built-in tools for creating charts and graphs, enabling users to build comprehensive statistical visualisations. When paired with Excel's suite of formatting capabilities, these visuals can be made exceptionally presentable and intelligible.

Additionally, Excel's VBA (Visual Basic for Applications) allows users to automate and execute complex operations, reinforcing Excel's stronghold in the finance and data analytics domain.

Excel also offers superior compatibility across various platforms, making it a tool that's easy to collaborate and share. It supports an array of file types, ensuring widespread accessibility and functionality.

Excel has anchored itself as an unrivaled tool in the management and analysis of information, especially in the finance sector. Owing to its user-friendly interface, robust functionalities, visual capabilities, and extensive compatibility, it's easy to grasp the staunch staying power of Excel.

Despite the rise of more advanced technologies like Python, understanding the strength of Excel reinforces its fundamental position in our toolkit. By acknowledging the power of Excel alongside Python, we are better equipped to harness the synergistic partnership between these two behemoths, for a holistic, efficient, and dynamic approach to data analysis. As we journey further into this exciting domain, the next pivot of our exploration awaits - Setting up the Python environment.

Setting Up the Python Environment

Steeling ourselves for the exciting quest that lies ahead, we turn our attention to a fundamental step- setting up Python on our system. This step functions as a launchpad for our journey into the intricate tapestry of Python and Excel, enabling us the necessary tools and systems to make our voyage successful and efficient.

The installation of Python typically begins with obtaining the python distribution from its official website. It's crucial to download the latest version of Python to make sure we're availing of the most recent features and performance improvements. Python, being an open-source language, is freely available for download across all significant platforms like Windows, MacOS, Unix, and other Linux variants.

Post download, you run the installer. At this point, it's prudent to check the box that says 'Add Python to PATH' before proceeding with the installation. This inclusion ensures that Python is added to your environment variables and is accessible from any command-line interface on your computer.

Now, comes a decision that largely depends on the user's preference - choosing an Integrated Development Environment (IDE) for Python. The IDE will essentially be your cockpit as you soar through the gratifying skies of Python programming. Popular IDEs include PyCharm, Eclipse, Atom, and Sublime Text. Selecting an IDE is subjective and should align with your comfort and the magnitude of the projects you aim to work on.

Post the installation of Python and an IDE, it's pivotal to install the necessary packages and libraries for data manipulation and computation. Packages such as NumPy, Pandas, SciPy, and Matplotlib form the backbone of the majority of data computational tasks and are thus essential.

How do you install packages and libraries, you might wonder? That's where PIP (Pip Installs Packages) steps in. PIP is a package management system that allows you to install and manage additional libraries and dependencies not packaged as part of the standard Python library. Just a simple command on your command-line interface allows you to install a drool-worthy repository of Python packages swiftly.

For integrating Python with Excel, you need the xlwings library. Xlwings is a Python library that makes writing and executing Python code in Excel uncomplicated, thereby, creating the bridge we require. A simple pip command on your command line i.e., 'pip install xlwings' will complete this necessary installation.

Finally, configuring xlwings with Excel is the finishing touch to our setup, and voila, you've successfully established your Python environment with Excel compatibility!

To fortify our upcoming expedition in Python and Excel, setting up an accommodating environment is the essential groundwork. From understanding the installation process and selecting the optimum Integrated Development Environment to knowing about indispensable Python packages, every step carves out our path and preempts possible obstacles.

The power of Python may seem reduced unless we can direct it well with sufficient preparatory work. As we set sail on this remarkable journey, the next cornerstone—a primer on the Python-Excel interface— awaits our attention. Armed with a sturdy foundation, let's move onto our next endeavor - understanding the operation of the xlwings interface for interlinking Python and Excel. Hold fast, as the ideal Python-Excel amalgamation is about to manifest into reality!

Navigating the Excel-Python Interface: An Introduction to xlwings

As we traverse into the enigmatic realm of Python and Excel integration, we find ourselves in need of a trusted guide to help us navigate the intriguing terrain. Fortunately, that guide is at hand - it comes in the form of an exceptional tool known as xlwings.

The crux of our journey entails exploiting the power of Python while retaining the familiarity and convenience of Excel. That is precisely where xlwings shines. Being a Python library, it allows us to use Python code to programmatically control virtually every aspect of Excel - from data manipulation and cleaning to executing advanced computations.

Let's start by invoking xlwings in an interpreter, after ensuring it's installed correctly (as outlined in the previous section). You will typically use the command 'import xlwings as xw', which imports the xlwings module under the alias 'xw'. This aliasing is a common practice in Python and serves to keep your code concise while enhancing readability.

With xlwings, interacting with Excel data from within Python feels natural. For instance, the command 'xw.Book('Book1')' would open an Excel workbook called 'Book1', and 'xw.sheets['Sheet1']' would allow access to a particular sheet in the workbook.

Reading and manipulating data with xlwings is no less effortless. If you have some data in cells A1 to C3 of your Excel sheet, 'xw.Range('A1:C3').value' would return the data in those cells as a nested list in Python. You could then manipulate that data using any Python function or method you like, before writing it back to an Excel range using the '.value' property.

Another compelling feature of xlwings is its ability to handle numpy arrays and pandas DataFrames natively. If you're dealing with larger datasets, you'd typically use pandas to conduct your data operations. With xlwings, you can read Excel data into a DataFrame using 'df = xw.Range('A1:C3').options(pd.DataFrame, index=False, header=True).value', manipulate the data using all the power of pandas, and write it back to Excel with a few simple commands.

Furthermore, xlwings also supports UDFs (User Defined Functions), which are Python-written functions that can run directly in Excel, much like traditional VBA (Visual Basic for Applications) functions. This allows for a level of flexibility and optimization that was previously only possible using VBA, significantly expanding the capabilities of what you can achieve with Excel-based data analysis and programming.

As we draw the curtains on our introduction to xlwings, one truth becomes glaringly apparent. When it comes to leveraging the combined capabilities of Python and Excel, xlwings is not just an interface - it's a beacon that illuminates the path to seamless integration.

Journeying through the xlwings landscape has equipped us with an understanding of how the library facilitates bridging the Python-Excel divide. These insights, in turn, arm us with the proficiency to embark on our exploration of where Python and Excel converge, illuminating use cases where they shine together in the next section.

From reading and manipulating Excel data using Python to handling pandas DataFrames natively and even developing and running Python functions directly in Excel as UDFs, the adaptability and potential applications of xlwings are indeed beguiling.

As we bestride the interface between Excel and Python, heralding new possibilities and coding horizons with xlwings, one thing is crystalline. We have reached an exciting turning point in our mission, one that inspires us to probe deeper and venture further into this riveting journey of Python for Excel. The upcoming sections are sure to harbor even more fascinating and enriching discoveries, so let's forge ahead with renewed fervor and an insatiable curiosity. The adventure is only just beginning!

Use Cases: Where Python and Excel Shine Together

As we charter into the topographies of potential Python and Excel synergies, we find ourselves not at the precipice of a cliff, but standing on the launchpad of exponential possibilities. The harmonic fusion of these platforms redefines limits, transcending boundaries, and launching us into fascinating frontiers of data navigation, exploration, and transformation.

There are limitless multitudes of scenarios where this unique amalgam of Python and Excel could be applied, focusing specifically on sectors where Excel can be augmented with Python's broad functionality arsenal, fueling greater efficiency, versatility, and depth.

In the sphere of data transformation and cleansing, Python accelerates the process exponentially. While Excel's native functions often struggle handling heavy data processing, Python, bolstered by libraries like Pandas, cleanses, wrangles, and converts large data sets with incredible efficiency.

Collaboratively, Excel's intuitive UI and Python's raw power form an ultra-effective data processing dynamo.

The realm of financial analytics, for instance, exposes another captivating scenario where Python and Excel integrate seamlessly. Leveraging Python's comprehensive scientific computation libraries like numpy and scipy, sophisticated financial models can be developed, applied, and evaluated directly within Excel workbooks. The inherent predictive capabilities of machine learning libraries, like sklearn, further enhance Excel-based financial forecasting models, driving unprecedented accuracy levels.

Let's now venture into the world of repetitive task automation. Herein lies another exemplary use case demonstrating the prowess of the Python-Excel partnership. Excel macros written in VBA often come with limitations, especially in interfacing with APIs or scraping websites. Python dives in as a savior, eliminating these barriers. Libraries such as BeautifulSoup and requests make possible the automation of data gathering and updating tasks inside Excel sheets that VBA can only dream of.

The chasm between Excel's data visualization capabilities and that demanded by today's data scientists and analysts can be bridged by Python libraries like Matplotlib, Seaborn, and Plotly. This integration enables the creation of far more complex, detailed, and interactive figures and charts within Excel - including 3D surface plots, cluster maps, and real-time data plots.

Furthermore, Excel's in-built limitations in performing statistical analysis can be triumphed over by Python's scipy and statsmodel libraries. It allows for more complex statistical operations like regression analysis, ANOVA, chi-square test, etc., to be executed directly within Excel.

Dragging our attention away from the resplendent entourage of application areas, a reality dawns upon us - the confluence of Python and Excel is not merely about broadening the possibilities of what we can do. Instead, it is the metamorphosis of how we perceive, approach, and unravel the labyrinth of data, opening new gateways to evolve our methodologies and strategies.

This moment in our Python for Excel odyssey marks a significant milestone as we stand at the crossroads of traditional methodologies and next-generation analytical capabilities. With a more profound understanding of where Python and Excel integrate to shine brightest, readers are now prepared to embrace the power of this fusion and harness it within their respective domains.

The upcoming chapters delve deeper into each of these application areas and more, taking readers on a guided expedition of integrating Python within their Excel workbooks. They promise a thrilling journey, filled with practical, hands-on demonstrations, invigorating insights, and paradigms altering perspectives. So, strap in, and get ready to dive into the exhilarating adventure that is Python for Excel.

Pre-requisites and What to Expect

As we stand on the threshold of our Python and Excel expedition, we need to ensure a meticulously designed roadmap and a well-stocked explorer's kit. This encompassing preparation, which includes the pre-requisites and expectations, acts as the heart of our journey, equipping you with the necessary tools, fortifying your understanding, and guiding you, at every step, towards your destination.

Before embarking upon our journey, it's of utmost importance to be aware of the pre-requisites. A comprehensive understanding of both Python and Excel is indispensable. As a well-versed explorer, be prepared to employ deep insights into Excel's intricacies, along with its tools, features, and functionalities at one hand, while adeptly maneuvering Python's versatile coding structures, data handling capabilities, and libraries at the other.

Additional prerequisites include a moderate understanding of VBA for Excel, especially for those intending to make a switch to Python from VBA. Besides, familiarity with Python IDEs would be helpful as the integration process heavily relies on tools like Jupyter Notebook, Spyder, or Google Colab. Basic knowledge of Python libraries like Numpy and Pandas is also paramount as they form the core of operations you will be executing in Excel.

By now, if you've already painted a picture of your journey, then let us delve deeper and set some expectations. 'Python for Excel Advanced: From CELL-FIEs to Financial Forecasts' is meticulously structured to offer a progressive growth experience. The book goes the extra mile to provide extensive knowledge on how Python can augment Excel's capabilities, within each section, emphasizing hands-on coding and real-life financial analysis examples.

Expect to confront a spectrum of topics and techniques, spanning from data cleansing with Pandas, automation using Python, in-depth data visualization, to even sophisticated financial modeling involving machine learning algorithms. In essence, the aim is to steer you towards mastering the art of integrating Python with Excel with such finesse that you seamlessly transition between the two, harnessing the best of both worlds.

Furthermore, this expedition is not just about conquering the Python-Excel landscape, but also about honing your skills to such an extent that they start to blend with your instincts. Hence, you can foresee a trajectory marked by numerous opportunities to learn, practical exercises, real-world applications, and absorbing demonstrations that motivate you to achieve new heights of proficiency at every juncture.

As we stand at the edge of our adventure, armed with our pre-requisites and illuminated by our set expectations, we're ready to embark to conquer this Python-Excel universe. Remember, each step you take forward equips you better for the looming challenges. While the journey will test your mettle, remember that the satisfaction of gaining mastery over integrating Python with Excel will be second to none.

This journey will wind through fascinating terrains, steep learning curves, surprise revelations, and numerous 'Aha!' moments. And it is this very uncertainty, this sense of adventure, that makes the Python and Excel integration a journey worth undertaking. You are now just a step away from the realm where finance meets programming—an idyllic paradise teeming with potent tools, powered by Excel and Python, awaiting your arrival. It's time to turn the page and begin this journey of exploration, learning, and infinite possibilities. Welcome aboard!

Limitations of Python and Excel Integration

While the union of Python and Excel has revolutionized data handling and financial analysis, it's important to recognize that every superhero does have their kryptonite. The integration of these two powerful tools is not without limitations. In this section, we'll expose the potential bottlenecks that may emerge in your journey, preparing you to navigate around these obstacles with deft agility and preparedness.

Amongst the most glaring limitations you'll confront is the reliance of Python on third-party libraries for integration with Excel. Libraries such as xlwings, pandas, openpyxl, among others, are what bridge Python with Excel, facilitating data manipulation, customization, and automation. However, the dependency on these libraries can become a hindrance. Their performance is often subjected to the maintenance and updates provided by their developers. An abandoned or poorly maintained library can strain your Python-Excel ecosystems with bugs, reduced efficiency, and compatibility issues, adding unexpected hitches to your workflow.

Another point of distress is the inherent difference between Python and Excel in handling data. While Excel is inherently designed for two-dimensional data with a rigid structure, Python, through Pandas, boasts the flexibility to handle multi-dimensional data. This difference might lead to unexpected results during complex data manipulation tasks involving dataframes with a highly nested structure.

Python and Excel also part ways when it comes to handling large datasets. Excel, due to its limited memory capacity, chokes when subjected to data beyond a certain size. Python, on the other hand, deals efficiently with large datasets, thanks to its proficient memory management. This limitation may constrain you to Python when working with extensive data, cutting Excel out of the scenario.

Another limitation to pay heed to is that Python, unlike Excel, requires an installed Python interpreter. For users who might not have the liberty to install software on their machines due to organizational restrictions or security concerns, this integration may become precarious.

Finally, the real-time execution characteristic of Excel macros gets blurred in Python, which prefers block execution of code crafted in external scripts. This difference impacts the functionality of event-triggered macros, an area where Excel unquestionably shines.

It's crucial to understand that every tool has its strengths and limitations. As an advanced user, your master stroke lies in intelligently leveraging the strengths and circumventing the weaknesses. Python and Excel are potent, but they are not the ultimate panacea. They tend to falter in certain domains, yet blaze a trail in others.

The limitations discussed underscore the fact that there is no 'one-size-fits-all' solution in the realm of data science and financial analysis. Python and Excel integration won't magically solve all your problems. Rather, it's an apparatus, another weapon in your armory that, when wielded with precision, can leave an indelible imprint on your financial conquests.

As we head into the next section, armed with the wisdom of the limitations and workarounds, let's enable ourselves to harness the true power of Python for Excel, exploiting the tools to their maximum potential while judiciously circumventing the challenges. It's the same as old adage goes: not all that glitters is gold, but a keen eye knows how to find the gold that doesn't glitter.

CHAPTER 2: FOUNDATIONS OF PYTHON PROGRAMMING FOR EXCEL USERS

Python Essentials for Excel Users

As an advanced user of Excel, you'd no doubt have encountered repetitive tasks that beg for automation or complex problems that cry out for a versatile solution. Enter Python—the swiss army knife of programming languages. Python, with its clear syntax, powerful libraries, and capacity to handle large datasets, forms an ideal companion to Excel. Let's embark on this dynamic journey, extending your already formidable Excel skills further with the potency of Python.

Python, in essence, is an interpreted, high-level, general-purpose programming language that is dynamically typed. Being high-level means that Python code is understandable by humans and does not require compilation before execution. Dynamic typing in Python supports flexibility, enabling you to switch variable types, such as swapping a string for a list in the same code block.

The beauty of Python's syntax is that it revolves around simplicity and readability. Python is structured using whitespace and tabulation, promoting code that is clean, well-organized, and easy to read. Features like these make Python an excellent introductory language even for beginners in programming. However, for Excel power users, Python extends an arsenal of advanced features and powerful libraries that open unparalleled avenues for data manipulation, analysis, and visualization.

A decisive factor that heralds Python among the top choices for Excel integration is its wide range of libraries and packages designed for data analysis and science. Prime examples are NumPy, Pandas, Matplotlib, and Scikit-learn. NumPy brings forth mathematical operations on arrays and matrices, a conventional sight in financial datasets. Pandas, akin to our trusted Excel, is superb with structured data manipulation, making it truly a savior in data wrangling tasks. It offers DataFrames – a data structure similar to Excel spreadsheets but considerably more powerful, offering methods for slicing, reshaping, merging, and pivoting data.

Further tooling includes Matplotlib and seaborn packages, our gateway to custom advanced data visualizations. These libraries, used alongside Pandas, help you create bar plots, histograms, scatter plots, and even more complex plots like pivot table heatmaps - right from within Python.

Furthermore, Python shines beyond Excel when it comes to machine learning. Via libraries like Scikit-learn, TensorFlow, and PyTorch, Python empowers you with advanced predictive modeling and decision-making tools. You can run regression analysis, classification algorithms, natural language processing, neural networks, and more at a level of complexity and sophistication unmatched in an Excel environment.

Python also features fantastic support for working with APIs and databases, making data integration and synchronization with Excel a breeze. Plus, Python offers scalable performance with larger datasets, a feat beyond Excel's capabilities.

How about we put this theory to test with a Python coding snippet? Below is an example of reading an Excel file using Pandas:

```
`  `

# Import packages
import pandas as pd

# Read an Excel file
df = pd.read_excel('financial_data.xlsx')

# Perform actions such as viewing the first five records
df.head()
`  `
```

This trivial piece of code can load an entire Excel worksheet into a Pandas DataFrame, opening the gates to use any of the powerful methods and functions that Pandas offers.

The aim is to make Excel users comfortable with Python, highlighting how familiar and powerful Python can be for regular Excel tasks and beyond. As we move deeper, we'll present more tailored Python functionality that intersects neatly with your Excel experience and significantly bolsters the data processing capabilities.

However, as we embark on this prodigious journey, it's essential to remember that Python isn't intended to replace Excel, but to complement it. The idea is not to always prefer Python over Excel or vice versa but to envisage a landscape where both exist, reinforcing each other's strengths. Some tasks are quicker and easier in Excel; others demand the flexibility and scalability of Python.

Excel continues to be an excellent tool for ad-hoc analysis, data entry, creating graphs quickly, or making reports with specific layouts. Still, once tasks become repetitive, require complex logic, or robust automation, Python comes bearing the torch, guiding you towards streamlined operations and amplified productivity.

The magic unfolds when Excel and Python play in tandem— an Excel spreadsheet as a front end, leveraging Python power in the back end. A paragon of this synergy is the xlwings library, which permits calling Python scripts from within Excel, directly linking Excel cells to Python functions. It forms the keystone of Python-Excel integration, as demonstrated in the coming sections.

As we gather these Python essentials and journey further, let's remember that the aim is not merely to learn Python, but to figure out how to leverage Python's power and potential to our advantage in an Excel-driven environment. Here, your prowess in Excel forms the foundation upon which we construct this bridge, blending the ease of Excel with the flexibility of Python, unraveling a perfect blend for advanced users ready to cross the bridge into a world full of possibilities.

Python, combined with Excel, manoeuvres beyond simple automation and ushers in an era of sophisticated data analysis, capable of impacting decision-making—the underlying goal of every financial analysis we undertake. Behold, for we are at the cusp of turning these possibilities into reality!

Integrating Python Code in Excel: An Overview of VBA-like Functionality

We've navigated through the essentials of Python, seen how it intertwines with our known Excel environment, and peeked at the power it holds. Now let's steer towards the harmony that Excel shares with Python — a unity that emerges through combining the user-friendly interface of Excel with the dynamic and flexible nature of Python to accomplish tasks far beyond the scope of each tool individually. Through this affiliation, we unlock the abilities of integrating Python code in an Excel environment, offering a panorama of VBA-like functionality but with superior power and versatility.

The principle behind Python-Excel integration is to interconnect two familiar environments and create a synergy where Python scripts work efficiently alongside Excel's interface. This combination enables users to create complex automated tasks, perform comprehensive data analysis, and ultimately make Excel an even more powerful tool.

The process generally resembles using VBA (Visual Basic for Applications) with Excel, but with Python as the scripting language being utilized. This provides a distinct advantage as Python offers readability, versatility, and comprehensive data manipulation and computational capabilities unmatched by VBA.

The journey of Python-Excel integration starts with the

xlwings library. xlwings is an open-source Python library that makes it straightforward to call Python from Excel and vice versa. It seamlessly integrates Python into Excel, thereby allowing you to use packages like NumPy and Pandas for numerical computations and data manipulation directly from Excel.

Let's demonstrate an instance of this integration with a simple Python function that takes values from Excel, performs computations, and outputs the results back into Excel. For instance, consider a Python function performing a simple arithmetic operation - a squaring function:

```python
import xlwings as xw

@xw.func
def square(num):
    return num ** 2
```

In a VBA-like fashion, this Python function, named `square`, can be called directly in Excel after being registered. If we type `=square(10)` in an Excel cell, it will call this Python function, and the cell will display the result `100`.

This brief example demonstrates a simple utilization. However, there's much more potential. More complex functions could involve constructing dynamic reports, applying machine learning models trained in Python onto Excel data, or automating data cleaning processes within Excel.

Python also holds an edge over VBA while dealing with larger datasets and performing complex computations, tasks that are cumbersome, or sometimes impossible, to execute in Excel alone. The ability to handle large and complex datasets, the availability of multitudes of libraries for a variety of tasks, and Python's ability to perform tasks quicker than VBA, qualify Python as a potent ally for Excel users.

Further, the possibilities don't stop there. Beyond xlwings, for even more advanced Python-Excel work, you can use Python to create User Defined Functions (UDFs), construct add-ins, and even build full applications that use Excel as a front end while Python performs the heavy lifting in the backend - creating a versatile system that balances Excel's accessibility with Python's computational strength.

Python within Excel takes us beyond basic automation, opens new vistas of data analytics, fosters better decision-making tools, and supercharges our financial data processing abilities - building, in essence, a robust data processing environment driven by the best of both worlds.

Working with Python IDEs

After immersing ourselves in the vibrant dynamics of Python-Excel integration, it's time we paid homage to the Python Interactive Development Environments (IDEs) - the unsung heroes where Python code comes to life. IDEs provide robust platforms where you can create, run and debug code, besides offering several advanced programming utilities. This section will explore these potent software suites, demystifying their features, and illuminating their pivotal role within our

Python for Excel advanced journey.

Python IDEs serve as an oasis for coders, providing a fortified environment brimming with code editing, debugging, automation, and much more. Some of the popular IDEs include PyCharm, Jupyter Notebook, Visual Studio Code, and Atom, among others. These integrated platforms bless coders with multifaceted capabilities, transforming abstract notions into operative code.

Let's consider the Jupyter Notebook – a stellar web-based IDE known for its interactive computing environment enabling the creation and sharing of documents that contain live code, equations, and visualizations. For our Excel-Python integration, Jupyter Notebook is particularly compelling given its ability to execute code in a cell-by-cell manner, maintaining the state of variables across these cells - a feature resembling Excel's cell structure.

To illustrate, let's take a brief Python code snippet that you could run in Jupyter Notebook:

```python
import pandas as pd

# Creating a Dataframe
df = pd.DataFrame({'A': ['foo', 'bar', 'foo', 'bar',
                'foo', 'bar', 'foo', 'foo'],
            'B': ['one', 'one', 'two', 'three',
                'two', 'two', 'one', 'three'],
            'C': np.random.randn(8),
            'D': np.random.randn(8)})
```

df

` ` `

The above script creates a pandas DataFrame that resembles an Excel spreadsheet. When run in a Jupyter cell, it outputs the DataFrame directly below the cell.

Another monumental Python IDE is PyCharm, a feature-rich, professional-grade IDE which stands as a paragon of the Python programming environment. Equipped with intelligent code assist, insightful debugging tools, and powerful search capabilities, PyCharm ensures rapid and efficient code development.

For instance, imagine you're dealing with a large codebase and want to debug a function that isn't behaving as expected:

` ` `python
def calculate_discount(price, discount_percent):
    discount = price * (discount_percent / 100)
    final_price = price - discount
    return final_price
` ` `

In PyCharm, you could drop a debugging point by simply clicking near the line number of a given line of code. Running the debugger, PyCharm stops at that point, allowing you to inspect variables, traverse code, and ensure your logic is being carried out as desired - an enormously helpful feature for building error-free, sophisticated Python applications.

Bearing in mind the grandeur of Python IDEs, the robustness

they bring to your Python-Excel journey, we should fully embrace their prowess. Whether it's the interactive environment of Jupyter Notebook simulating a dynamic cell-by-cell workflow or PyCharm's high-grade programming environment, IDEs are invaluable comrades guiding us through our Python expedition.

As we advance, remember: Success, while integrating Python with Excel, is not only about understanding Python syntax or Excel's interface but also about effectively employing the right tools like Python IDEs that hoist your coding productivity and efficiency to unheralded heights.

The Python for Excel advanced journey demands you to not just become adept at Python programming or navigating through Excel spreadsheet labyrinth, but to conquer these brilliant integrated development environments – to code, debug, and produce with exceptional power that only Python IDEs can provide. Forge ahead, my fellow Excel warriors and Python aficionados, let these Python IDEs be your guiding stars.

Python's Standard Library

Levelling up in our Python for Excel adventure, we turn our attention to an unsung powerhouse - Python's Standard Library. In the vast panorama of Python's features, the Standard Library remains one of the language's most attractive propositions. This repository of pre-coded modules enriches Python's statute considerably, allowing us to perform a multitude of operations right out-of-the-box. Hence, understanding its profound potential is vital to our Python-Excel journey.

Python's Standard Library, a grand entourage of stellar pre-included tools, caters to a vast assortment of programming needs. Whether you need to interact with the Internet, perform complex mathematical operations, or process XML data, Python's Standard Library has you covered.

Let's consider our Python-Excel point of view. There are numerous ways Python's Standard Library supports our cause. For example, the csv module, a highly versatile toolkit present in the Standard Library, can read and write CSV files, potentially bridging your Excel data with a Python environment.

Here's an example of how Python's csv module can read data from an existing excel file:

```python
import csv

with open('my_excel_data.csv', 'r') as f:
    reader = csv.reader(f)
    for row in reader:
        print(row)
```

This short and simple script opens a CSV file ('my_excel_data.csv') and iterates through each row, displaying them as Python lists. The csv reader converts each row of the CSV file into a list, which we can manipulate within Python effortlessly.

Furthermore, Python's Standard Library also boasts other Excel-related modules such as json, a module for Json data manipulation that assists in converting JSON data (a common format for web data) into a Pythonic data structure. This is particularly beneficial for Excel users venturing into data analysis involving API-sourced data.

```python
import json

# Convert a Json string to Python object
user = json.loads('{"id": 9, "name": "John", "tags": ["Python", "Excel"]}')
# Now 'user' is a Python dictionary
```

Another noteworthy constituent of Python's Standard Library benefiting our Python-Excel journey is the math module. If you deal with complex mathematical operations in Excel, you would appreciate Python's math module, offering a vast array of mathematical functionalities.

```python
import math

# Calculate factorial
print(math.factorial(5))
# Output: 120
```

In this snippet, we import Python's math module to calculate the factorial of 5 - an operation beyond Excel's native capabilities without additional VBA scripts.

Accentuating Python's diverse feature set, its Standard Library exemplifies Python's underlying principle - 'Batteries Included'. It amplifies the capabilities of Python, making it a versatile and powerful language ideal not just for Excel integration, but a plethora of additional functionalities.

An essential premise to echo in our Python-Excel journey is that remember, while Python's syntax or Excel's interface forms the bedrock, tools like Python's Standard Library bring wings to your coding endeavours, conquering the sky of potential Python-Excel synergies.

So, whether it be common programming tasks or difficult challenges, take a moment to explore the Sterling Standard Library. It just might provide the tools you need, all in the comfort of Python's own backyard. Always remember, every step with Python's Standard Library nudges you closer to the zenith of Python-Excel prowess.

Python Data Structures for Excel

Journeying further into the heartland of Python, we now encounter a significant milestone, the power-cogs that keep Python machinery running smoothly - Python's data structures. In our pursuit of seamless Python-Excel integration, understanding these indispensable structures is inescapable. Leveraging Python's data structures unlocks the potential to manage, manipulate and compute large volumes of data, making them especially useful for advanced Excel users, let's unfold this intriguing chapter.

Python's data structures, broadly segregated into built-ins like lists, dictionaries, sets, and tuples and advanced structures like arrays, dataframes, and series, lay the foundation of data organization in Python.

Consider Python lists, a built-in, mutable, and heterogeneous data structure capable of storing an ordered collection of items. Its mutable nature offers the flexibility to change its content even after its creation, offering promising applications in Excel where manipulation of cell data reflects in real-time.

```python
# A Python List
items = ['Apple', 'Banana', 'Cherry']
# Update an item
items[1] = 'Blueberry'
```

In this example, we form a list 'items' and replace 'Banana' with 'Blueberry'. Like filling cells in an Excel row, we filled our Python list - but with much greater flexibility to manipulate.

Another fundamental Python data structure is the dictionary, an unordered, dynamic, and mutable structure. Dictionaries in Python act similarly to Excel's VLOOKUP functionality - data are stored in key-value pairs, with keys providing unique access to each value.

```python
```

```python
# A Python Dictionary
fruit_colors = {'Apple': 'Red', 'Banana': 'Yellow', 'Cherry': 'Red'}
# Get color of Banana
print(fruit_colors['Banana'])
# Output: Yellow
```

In this example, 'Apple', 'Banana', and 'Cherry' are keys, each linked to a unique colour, their value. This dictionary mimics an Excel scenario where we map our data, such as an index matched with specific values.

Moving towards more advanced realms, we reach Pandas, a Python library offering powerful data structures like DataFrames and Series, ideal for analytics and data manipulations in Excel. To extract Excel data, organise it, or compute, you'll find DataFrames and Series invaluable.

```python
import pandas as pd

# Create a DataFrame
df = pd.DataFrame({
    'Fruit': ['Apple', 'Banana', 'Cherry'],
    'Color': ['Red', 'Yellow', 'Red'],
})

# Similar to Excel cell reference: Get color of fruit in the second row
print(df.loc[1,'Color'])
# Output: Yellow
```

` ` `

In this snippet, we mimic an Excel sheet with Pandas DataFrame, where 'Fruit' and 'Color' form columns, each filled with corresponding items. Perform Excel functions like pivot, filter, and lookup will seem more intuitive and efficient than ever when using these Panda structures.

Diving into Python's data structures provides insight into how Python elevates data manipulation exercise, matching and often surpassing Excel's abilities. Python's inherent data structures like lists and dictionaries, coupled with advanced structures from libraries like pandas, pave the way for endless possibilities of intricate data manipulations that we thought were exclusive to Excel.

Embedded in Python's data structures lie the keys to broader horizons in your Python-Excel journey. Harnessing these power structures not only catalyses your coding abilities but also encourages you to introspect the limitations of Excel sheets and venture beyond - into the realm of large-scale data manipulations and analysis.

And so, across the threshold of Python data structures, we move into the realm of modules and libraries, where Python's magic deepens.

Python Modules and Libraries

Python modules and libraries are like prefabricated building blocks that save you from reinventing the wheel. They encompass extensive utility functions, data structures, and classes, each designed to address specific programming requirements.

Consider the case of Python's Standard Libraries - a rich offering of modules that come bundled with Python. These cover a diverse range of functionalities, from file I/O, mathematical operations, internet data handling, to data persistence and manipulation.

```python
# Using the csv module from the Standard Library to read a
CSV file - an Excel File format.
import csv
with open('file.csv', 'r') as file:
    reader = csv.reader(file)
    for row in reader:
        print(row)
```

In the example above, Python's csv module reads and prints each row from an Excel CSV file. Not only it keeps the code clean and concise but also, efficient and effective.

In Python, specialised external libraries often play a critical role. For instance, the Pandas library, which extends Python's native capabilities of data manipulation and analysis, making it more compatible and comparable to Excel's analytical power.

```python
# Pandas' powerful data manipulation capabilities
import pandas as pd
df = pd.read_csv('file.csv')
print(df.head())
```

` ` `

With just three lines of code, Pandas not only reads the CSV file but also promptly displays the first five records, all thanks to the .head() function that it encapsulates.

Python's SciPy library is another heavy hitter for Excel users looking to extend their reach beyond native Excel capabilities. It offers mathematical functions, optimization routines, and statistical functions much more advanced than Excel's.

Integration of such libraries and modules into your Excel toolkit can seriously augment your possibilities of data manipulation, management, and analysis, in turn widening your realm of capabilities.

A stride through Python's modules and libraries offers a glimpse into Python's celebrated versatility. It is this that allows Python to integrate seamlessly with Excel to form a powerful combination. By understanding and leveraging the capabilities of these Python extensions such as libraries and modules, we can overcome many limitations and frustrations commonly encountered in Excel.

The Two Titans: Python and VBA for Excel - A Comparative Study

To compare Python and VBA for Excel, we must first comprehend that they originate from the different programming paradigms. Python, born in an open-source environment, continues to evolve with the contributions of its global community, fostering flexibility and growth. In contrast, VBA - Visual Basic for Applications, a proprietary coding language of Microsoft, is intrinsically integrated within the Office suite, offering native interactivity with Excel,

Word, and other Office applications.

One of the significant strengths of VBA for Excel is its seamless integration and the ease of automating tasks within Excel. Whether it is creating macros, manipulating Excel objects, or creating custom Excel functions, VBA provides a simple and straightforward way of achieving these tasks.

```vba
' A simple VBA code to input data in a cell
Sub InputData()
Range("A1").Value = "Hello, Excel!"
End Sub
```

In this quick example, the VBA code inputs data into an Excel cell without an intermediary like a Python Excel library. This kind of seamless manipulation is more accessible in VBA for Excel.

However, when it comes to complex data analysis, mathematical libraries, web scraping, and machine learning, Python races ahead of VBA. Python's extensive selection of libraries such as Numpy, Pandas, Matplotlib, Scipy, and Sklearn, positions it as a powerful tool for data science, econometrics, and financial modeling.

```python
# A simple Python code using Pandas for data manipulation.
import pandas as pd
df = pd.read_excel('sample.xlsx')
df['new_column'] = df['A'] + df['B']
```

` ` `

In only three lines of code, Python reads an Excel file and performs data manipulation using Pandas, which integrates seamlessly with Excel ensuring effective and efficient data analysis.

Another crucial advantage of Python over VBA is its superior error handling and debugging facilities, making your programming journey more comfortable. Python's syntax is also cleaner and more straightforward compared to VBA's, thereby enhancing code readability and maintainability.

The comparison of Python and VBA for Excel illuminates the fact that each has its unique strengths. When we integrate these two titanic forces, we gain a powerful toolset tailored for advanced Excel use, harnessing the benefits of both programming languages. As we stride forward in our Python-Excel journey, it is this synthesis that we endeavour to master, intertwining the simplicity and power of Python with the native functionality of VBA.

As an Advanced Excel user, contemplating an overlay of Python's and VBA's capabilities can unlock a comprehensive and powerful toolkit that can cater to complex requirements.

The terrain of our Python for Excel quest may be rough, and the journey strenuous, but we've got Python and VBA to accompany us, two governors of their realms. So, equipped with these insights about Python and VBA, are you ready to delve deeper? Up next, we explore the intriguing world of data manipulation and cleaning with Python and Excel. **Join us as we uncover the next chapter of our thrilling saga...**

CHAPTER 3: DATA MANIPULATION AND CLEANING WITH PYTHON AND EXCEL

Importing and Exporting Data

Welcome to the 3rd chapter of our exploration of the confluence of Python and Excel. We stand poised at a key juncture in our journey, ready to traverse the realm of data manipulation and cleaning. Importing and exporting data form the foundation of this expedition, constituting the lifeblood of our financial analysis and modelling. Adept management of these actions will catalyse our larger quest, unlocking avenues for deeper and richer exploration into advanced Python and Excel functionalities.

Understanding how data moves between the Python environment and Excel is crucial for any advanced user. The process encompasses two critical operations: absorbing data into Python from an Excel workbook—known as importing —and conversely, expelling data from Python into an Excel workbook—fondly referred to as exporting. These operations form the vital gateway of information inflow and outflow.

Let's kick off by understanding how Python interacts with Excel files. Python's open-source libraries such as 'pandas' and 'xlrd' grant Python the ability to read Excel files. Now our Excel data is not limited to static tables; it can be leveraged to perform an entire spectrum of operations in the conducive Python environment.

```python
# Python code to import Excel data using pandas
import pandas as pd
df = pd.read_excel('sample.xlsx') # Reads the whole excel file
```

This piece of Python magic can easily import data from any Excel workbook into your Python environment in the form of a DataFrame. This is Python's way of interpretation data tables. DataFrames are incredibly flexible and are particularly useful for working with statistical data.

Exporting data from Python to Excel is hardly a bone-breaker either. All the refined and transformed data in Python can be efficiently exported to Excel to create readable, shareable reports or perform further analysis.

```python
# Python code to export data into an Excel file
df.to_excel('output.xlsx', index = False)    # Exports the DataFrame to an excel file
```

Running this code will save a newly minted Excel file, named 'output.xlsx', adorned with the DataFrame's data in the same directory.

What's even better is that Python can support exporting to multiple sheets, or even various Excel files at once. The functionality extends beyond simple data, handling formulas and advanced Excel functions, generating dynamically updated Excel workbooks. The power unleashed when merging Python's data processing capabilities with Excel's flexibility and familiarity is truly prodigious.

We've now peered through the gateway of information import and export. Our Python-Excel palette colors with importing Excel files into Python, performing data manipulation, and then exporting the data back into Excel. Armed with this ability, you're now ready for any task—be it organizing your data, fixing inconsistencies, creating reports, or feeding prepared data into statistical models.

Sprinkling Python into the Excel world opens up new dialogues of conversation between your data and you. Our journey into the Python-Excel kingdom inches forward as we dive deeper into the heart of Python data manipulation.

Feel the magnificence of the power encompassed within Python and Excel at your fingertips. We promise, your data will thank you. As we inch further into the expansive panorama of Data Manipulation with Python and Excel, the herald of the new chapter — Cleaning and Transforming Data — beckons. "**Onward, we quest!**". **Next up, Cleaning and Transforming Data.** This topic is the next gate to conquer in our expedition, so affix the helmet and prepare for a dive into the data trenches.

Cleaning and Transforming Data

As we delve further into the ocean that is Python Excel integration, we reach some rough yet pivotal waves - tackling data cleaning and transformation. These processes constitute the potter's wheel that will shape our raw clay - the imported data - into a magnificent artefact, ready for high-quality analysis or forecast modelling. To put it simply, without effective data cleaning and transformation, any downstream analysis or modelling process is akin to building a skyscraper on quicksand.

The smooth sailing into the Python-Excel world starts to encounter slightly choppier waters as we discuss the essential steps of data preparation - cleaning and transformation. Duplication, inconsistency, missing values are tiny demons that can lead our analysis or forecasts astray. Hence, sanitising data – removing duplicates and inconsistencies, dealing with missing values – is a crucial ceremonial purification before proceeding.

Let's start with data cleaning. Python's pandas library offers some incredible tools for this. Here's an example of identifying and removing duplicates.

```python
# Python code to find and remove duplicates
df.duplicated()   # Checks for duplicate rows
df.drop_duplicates() # Drops duplicate rows
```

In the process of cleaning, often one comes across missing data. It's up to our discretion to fill in these gaps with an educated guess or to leave them empty. Here's an example of filling missing data.

```python
# Python code to fill missing values
df.fillna(0)   # Fills missing data with 0s
```

Now let's navigate through the waters of data transformation. Transforming data involves changing the scale or format of the data to make it suitable for further analysis. Here's an example of standardising the data to a standard normal distribution.

```python
# Python Code for Standardisation
from sklearn.preprocessing import StandardScaler
scaler = StandardScaler()
df = pd.DataFrame(scaler.fit_transform(df), columns = df.columns)
```

The beauty of Python and pandas is that it allows us to clean and transform data almost effortlessly, ensuring that the data is prepped and primed for any type of advanced Excel functionality or analysis that might follow.

More than Aesthetics: The Consequences of Purified Data

We've tackled the daemons of duplicates and inconsistencies, and soared over the hurdle of missing values, painting a clearer picture with our data. We've transformed our data to suit our vision of understanding, making it easier for us to digest in-depth analysis or forecast models.

The price of not valuing data cleaning and transformation might be steep, with the end result being inaccurate and misleading. On the contrary, well-cleaned and transformed data are strong pillars that can hold the weight of even the heaviest analysis or complex models.

Data Exploration and Visualization

Data cleaning and transformation is akin to treasure hunting—meticulously cleaning and polishing the artefacts to shine brilliantly in their full glory. But the hunt doesn't stop there. Now that the treasure is sparkling clean and transformed into a format we can better understand, the time comes to examine it closely and take note of all its intricate details—that is where data exploration and visualization come into play.

Data exploration is one of the most fascinating steps in data analysis. It invites us into an explorative journey into uncharted facets of our dataset, uncovering patterns and trends, outliers, and unexpected results that might have been missed. This is where Python paired with Excel exhibits its sheer prowess.

To begin our exploration, Python provides libraries such as pandas for detailed analysis and numpy for numerical computation, that helps to dive deep and elicit insights from our data. Here's a simple example of summarising your data with Python's pandas:

```python
```

```
# Python code to describe data
df.describe()    # Summarize the central tendency, dispersion
and shape of a dataset's distribution
` ` `
```

The summarize function gives you a snapshot of your data's overall distribution, computing various statistical metrics such as mean, median, and standard deviation. But sometimes numbers alone can not paint the full picture. Here is where data visualization adds colour to our understanding.

Data visualization is the graphic representation of data which involves producing images that communicate relationships among the data for easier understanding. Python shines here with libraries such as Matplotlib and Seaborn.

An example of a histogram, representing the frequency distribution of a continuous data column using Matplotlib is shown below:

```python
# Python code for histogram
import matplotlib.pyplot as plt
df['column_name'].plot(kind='hist', rwidth=0.8)
plt.show()
` ` `
```

The resultant histogram allows us quick identification of trends and distributions across our dataset. It provides a visual representation that often makes complex data more understandable and usable. This information, once locked away in rows and columns of numerical values, can now be easily interpreted at a glance, augmenting our understanding and streamlining the decision-making process.

Visuals speak louder than words. By exploring and visualizing our data, we've generated a realm of patterns, correlations, and trends that narrate the whispering tales of our data. We've turned the monolith of numbers into a canvas of meaningful visuals, which, unlike naked datasets, don't befuddle the viewer, instead present the concealed information with instant clarity.

The power of data exploration and visualization could be transformational, influencing the rapidity and precision of the decision-making process. The tale of numbers gets told in the language of visuals, leading to an insightful narrative waiting to be heeded.

Regular Expressions for Data Cleaning

As we tread on our data journey, it becomes essential to have clean, high-quality data because any analysis or visualisation is as good as the raw material it is built upon. Here, we anchor at the shores of regular expressions, an indispensable tool for data cleaning. This powerful formal language has mastery over string pattern searching and manipulation, forming an essential skill in any data aficionado's toolkit.

Imagine you are a detective, and the raw data set is the case you have to crack. Regular expressions are like the magnifying glass that helps intricately sift through the data, scrutinising each string to find matching patterns or discrepancies.

Known as 'regex', these character sequences enable us to find patterns in our data instead of just exact matches. Python, with its 're' library, supports the formulation of a regex within a Python script and is particularly handy for text processing.

Let us look at an example, say, isolating email addresses from a text:

```python
# Python code for Regular Expression
import re

text = 'For more details, mail us at info@pythonforexcel.com and sales@pythonforexcel.com'
emails = re.findall(r'[\w\.-]+@[\w\.-]+', text)

for email in emails:
    print(email)
```

In the code above, `findall()` function returns all non-overlapping matches of the pattern in a string as a list of strings. The string is scanned from left to right, and matches are returned in the order found. If one or more groups are present in the pattern, it returns a list of groups.

We see that the regular expression pattern `[\w\.-]+@[\w\.-]+` is created to match any characters ranging from a-zA-Z, any number 0-9, a dot or a hyphen, preceding an @ symbol and following it, isolating the email addresses.

This invaluable functionality can cleanse data, extract pertinent details, and even transform the data to a more desirable format.

But one must appreciate that the strength of regex can also be its weakness. Its capacity for executing complex pattern recognition also results in equally intricate syntax which can feel daunting to newcomers. However, with patience and practice, harnessing this power can open up new data vistas to explore and analyze.

Nurturing Precision: The Prominence of Regular Expression in Data Cleaning

With regular expression aboard our data journey, we gain formidable allies in establishing pattern recognition and string manipulation. Regex becomes the scalpel that delicately incises unwanted elements or the thread that seamlessly mends tattered sections of our dataset.

What once seemed like an overwhelming deluge of data now is a purified stream, cleaned, decluttered and transformed into the right format. This cleaning process paves the way towards a more efficient and unobstructed path to interpretation, understanding, and decision making.

Advanced Data Filtering

Every data analyst knows that traversing the data landscape isn't a straight path, but a journey filled with turns and twists. Not every piece of data is equal; some bear valuable insights while others may lead down a spiral of confusion. Hence, one needs advanced filtering tools to dim the noise and amplify the signals.

Python, with its wealth of libraries, offers one such advanced filtering tool, the Pandas library. Combining flexibility and high performance, Pandas transforms the way we explore and manipulate our data sources.

Let's glance at how advanced data filtering unfolds with Python. In this example, we filter financial data for a specific range:

```python
import pandas as pd

# Load data
df = pd.read_csv('financial_data.csv')

# Define Filters
filter_profit = df['Profit'] > 10000
filter_loss = df['Loss'] < -5000

# Apply Filters
filtered_df = df.where(filter_profit & filter_loss)
```

In the example above, we first import the necessary Pandas library and load our financial data using the `read_csv()` function. We then define the criteria for our filters, where we want to isolate entries with a profit greater than 10,000 and a loss less than -5000. Finally, we apply these filters to our data using the `where()` function, which returns a DataFrame of the same shape, but with entries that do not meet the filter criteria replaced with NaN.

Thanks to Python's numpy-powered Pandas library, filtering data becomes a matter of defining the right filter conditions and applying them to our DataFrame with an intuitive, high-level interface.

Remember, it's not always about the data you gather, but it's about the information you elucidate from the data that drives decisions. Advanced data filtering techniques hand you the navigation controls, enabling you to steer towards the most insightful parts of your dataset.

Validating Data Integrity

Like a jeweler verifying the authenticity of a diamond, a data analyst must ensure that the data under analysis is untainted, accurate and holistic - in essence, ensuring data integrity. The world of Python, with its substantial toolbox, opens up an array of strategies to examine the quality and validity of our data.

Data integrity alludes to the accuracy, consistency, and reliability of data over its life-cycle. This compass of truth involves maintaining the physical accuracy of data, ensuring no unauthorized alterations occur, and verifying that the data is reliable and can be trusted for decision-making.

Ensuring data integrity in Python starts from the initial stages of data import itself. Python's Pandas library offers several data validation techniques, including built-in functions to handle missing data, duplicate data, and erroneous values.

A common technique applied during data validation in Python is the use of assertion statements. Assertion in Python is an aid in debugging, where we define a condition and assert that it holds true. If the condition evaluates as True, the program continues undisturbed, if False, the program stops and throws an AssertionError.

Here is a brief example of an assertion check in Python to validate that there are no missing values in our data:

```python
import pandas as pd

# Load data
df = pd.read_csv('financial_data.csv')

# Assert that there are no missing values
assert pd.notnull(df).all().all()
```

In the code snippet above, we first import the Pandas library and load our financial data. The `assert` statement is used to ensure that there are no missing values in the data. The inner `all()` function checks that all column values are True for the function `notnull()`, which evaluates whether a value is non-missing. The outer `all()` is a further aggregation that checks across all columns.

However, data integrity is not just about handling missing or erroneous values; it is a spectrum that includes maintaining the completeness and accuracy of data.

Effective data validation is a gatekeeper to reliable insights. When the gates of integrity remain unbreached, data showcases its potential to steer significant business decisions and be a dependable cornerstone for innovation.

Reliable data is akin to an artist's signature - validating the assurances claimed, providing attribution and fostering trust. It remains a pivotal factor in creating a reliable analysis, prediction model, or an AI tool. Just as an artist's credibility grows with each validated masterpiece, so does the reliability of a data analysis model with maintained data integrity.

Unrolling the map of further exploration, we find ourselves amidst 'Batch Processing in Excel with Python,' the awaiting trail in our Python for Excel journey. The probabilities of achieving higher efficiency in data processing invite us. With enlightened minds and eager hearts, let's continue our voyage. The ocean of exploration never dries up; it ever widens with the expanding horizons of knowledge.

Batch Processing in Excel with Python

Like the power of a symphony in which multiple instruments play in harmony to create a beautiful melody, successful data analysis often necessitates the orchestration of multiple tasks performed smoothly and simultaneously. One strategy to achieve this in the realm of data analysis and processing is batch processing. This approach, driven by Python's powerful capabilities when integrated with Excel, can significantly enhance efficiency, reduce manual effort, and free up resources for other crucial tasks.

Batch processing is an execution of a series of tasks in a program non-interactively. It essentially means running 'batches' of tasks as a group rather than individually, harnessing the power of automation and delivering outputs more efficiently.

Python brings its versatility and power to batch processing in

Excel, where it can automate time-consuming tasks, handle large datasets, and perform complicated computations. The `pandas` and `openpyxl` libraries, for instance, work in unison to read, manipulate and write data to Excel files, presenting a massive improvement in efficiency compared to manually modifying Excel data.

To delve into an illustrative example, let's consider a situation where you need to apply specific transformations to a multitude of excel spreadsheets. You could either go the conventional route and manually process each file or choose the Python way and automate the task.

Let's write a simple Python batch processing script using `pandas` and `glob`, a library that allows Python to work with files effectively:

```python
import pandas as pd
import glob

def process_files():
    # Gather all Excel files from the directory
    files = glob.glob('./*.xlsx')

    for file in files:
        # Read in each file
        data = pd.read_excel(file)

        # Apply transformations
        data = data[data['Revenue'] > 10000] # Filter rows where 'Revenue' is more than 10000
```

```
    # Save transformed files
    data.to_excel(file, index=False)

process_files()
```

In the code snippet above, the script first uses `glob` to gather all Excel files in the current directory. It then iterates over each file, reads the data into a DataFrame, and applies the transformation - filtering rows based on a condition. The transformed DataFrame is then written back to the Excel file, ensuring that all files in the directory are processed in one fell swoop.

As this chapter draws to a close, it leaves us with the powerful concept of batch processing, a potential game-changer in the realm of data manipulation and cleaning. It's the maestro who harmonizes the operations, elucidates the rhythm of computing, allows us to compose the grand symphony of our data narrative.

The beauty and strength of batch processing lie in its capability to replace several individual steps with a single, efficient operation. It holds the potential to transform an analyst's interaction with Excel, allowing for seamless manipulation, cleaning, and transformation of substantial amounts of data. With Python as the orchestrator, Excel morphs from a simple instrument into a member of a harmonized, modern symphony.

CHAPTER 4:
ADVANCED EXCEL FUNCTIONS AND MACROS WITH PYTHON

Extending Excel's Functionality

Just as a master sculptor transforms a block of marble into a work of art, Python can significantly expand the capabilities of Excel, turning this popular spreadsheet application into a dynamic and robust data manipulation tool. The piece of marble hereby represents Excel's existing capabilities, and Python is the gifted sculptor, capable of molding and adding intricate details into the block, enhancing its aesthetics, and increasing its grandeur.

Python can take Excel's functionality beyond its standard borders, integrating comprehensive capabilities that aren't built into Excel. These range from complex calculations and data analysis to machine learning and advanced visualizations, all while providing more efficient and accelerated processing power.

Python does this by tapping into several robust libraries that help improve Excel, such as NumPy for numerical computations, Pandas for data manipulation and analysis, Matplotlib for creating plots and visualizations, and many others.

Consider an Excel workbook with continuous data streaming in real-time. Excel's built-in functionalities may not be able to cope with the complexity and pace of real-time data analysis and visualization. But when Python steps into the picture, you could use libraries like Plotly for real-time data visualization or Twisted for networking and real-time processing.

For instance, if you have a data-streaming application that accrues critical data, continuously filling the Excel workbook, you could use Python to automatically produce essential insights and real-time visualizations ending up with dynamic, effective dashboards. Here's a simple example of how you could use Python's Pandas and Plotly libraries to achieve real-time updates in your Excel dashboard.

```python
import pandas as pd
from plotly.subplots import make_subplots
import plotly.graph_objects as go
from plotly.offline import plot

# Read in dataset (real-time data stream)
data = pd.read_excel('real_time_data.xlsx')

# Creating subplot with time series
```

```
fig = make_subplots(rows=2, cols=1)

# Create time series scatter plot
fig.add_trace(go.Scatter(x=data.index, y=data['Temperature'],
                mode='lines',
                name='Temperature'),
        row=1,
        col=1)

# Create bar chart
fig.add_trace(go.Bar(x=data.index,          y=data['Humidity'],
name='Humidity'),
            row=2,
            col=1)

# Update xaxis properties
fig.update_xaxes(title_text='Time', row=1, col=1)

# Update yaxis properties
fig.update_yaxes(title_text='Temperature', row=1, col=1)
fig.update_yaxes(title_text='Humidity', row=2, col=1)

# Update title and height
fig.update_layout(title_text='Real-time Data Analysis with
Python and Excel', height=700)

# Generate HTML file
plot(fig)
```
```
```

In the above script, the code reads an Excel worksheet with real-time data, whereafter Plotly generates real-time visualizations, fetching the live data and updating the graphs (for this example, temperature and humidity readings over time) accordingly.

View Excel not as a single entity, but rather as a spectrum that Python can enrich. Each aspect of Excel that Python enhances is a new color added to this spectrum, resulting in a radiant, comprehensive tool capable of tackling an array of challenges.

Integrating Python with Excel opens doors to previously unexplored functionalities, resulting in an elevated, more flexible Excel ecosystem. It's Python's versatility and adaptive nature that gives it an edge over Excel's VBA, rendering capabilities that are beyond Excel's original design and specification. It provides the agility to shift smoothly between simple spreadsheets and complex data analysis tasks.

Automating Repetitive Tasks

The definition of insanity, as famously quoted by Albert Einstein, is doing the same thing over and over again and expecting different results. In Excel, tedious and repetitive tasks can feel just like that - insanity. But fear not, for Python is our valiant knight, radiating hope and shining light in the dungeons of monotony.

Python, with its intuitive syntax and powerful libraries, is like an orchestra conductor, seamlessly managing and coordinating the repetitive processes within Excel, enabling you to perform repetitive tasks automatically, thus saving you both time and effort and reducing the risk of human error.

To demonstrate the power of Python in automating Excel tasks, let's consider a common use case: consolidating multiple Excel files into one. Depending on the number of files, manually doing this can be extremely laborious.

Here is an example of how Python can come to the rescue:

```python
import os
import pandas as pd

dir_path = "C:/Users/Name/Documents/Excel_files/"
merged_file = "merged_excel.xlsx"

files = [f for f in os.listdir(dir_path) if f.endswith(".xlsx") or f.endswith(".xls")]

data_frames = [pd.read_excel(dir_path + f) for f in files]

merged_df = pd.concat(data_frames, ignore_index=True)

merged_df.to_excel(dir_path + merged_file)
```

In the script above, Python first recognizes all Excel files in a specified directory. It then reads each file into a pandas DataFrame. Python finally merges all data frames and writes the resulting DataFrame into a new Excel file. This entire process is done in seconds, thus saving you countless hours of manual labor.

Not stopping here, Python can automate a plethora of tasks, ranging from data cleaning and processing, creating and applying formulas, conducting batch operations, creating charts, exporting data, and much more.

Moreover, by leveraging Python in conjunction with Excel, you can automate tasks that involve not just Excel but other resources as well, such as databases, APIs, other software tools, and even other Excel files. This flexibility allows Python to be an excellent tool for creating end-to-end automation solutions.

Automation in Excel with Python is like a magical incantation that extends your reach and amplifies your endeavors. A repetitive task, which could take hours if done manually, can be automated, allowing it to run in minutes or even seconds while you could focus on more productive or creative tasks.

But the power of automation with Python expands beyond just Excel. It opens up the possibility of creating more extensive automation solutions by integrating Excel with other applications and services, thereby resulting in an overall increased efficiency and productivity. In other words, you can stand on Python's shoulders to extend your reach, touching the vast horizons of possibilities that Excel has to offer.

Working with Advanced Excel Formulas

As a connoisseur of the symphony composed by the harmony of Python and Excel, the elementary ways of Excel formula manipulation may seem child's play to you. It is now time to don your diving suit and take a plunge into the profound depths of advanced Excel formulas.

Excel is indeed an alchemist's tool, manipulating raw data into precious wisdom, all achieved through the magic of formulas. And when these intricate formulas are orchestrated by Python, you can bequeath the Midas touch to your datasets, transforming numbers into solid gold insights.

Understanding advanced Excel formulas requires familiarity with both Excel's inherent functionality and Python's capabilities in handling them. The marriage of Python's Xlwings library and Excel's functionalities creates a band that plays harmonious chords of automation.

Xlwings facilitates interaction with Excel's built-in functions and user-defined formulas in an easy yet powerful way. While Excel's native realm of formulas covers an extensive ground, encompassing mathematical models, statistical functions, financial computations and array operations, harnessing them through Python amplifies their potency to a prodigious extent.

Consider the case when you want to apply a complex array formula across an expansive range. With Python directing the operation, it is as simple as writing a few lines of code:

```python
import xlwings as xw

book = xw.Book('workbook.xlsx')
sheet = book.sheets['Sheet1']

# Define range to place the formula
rng = sheet.range('B2:B100')
```

```
# Write the array formula into the first cell
rng.api.FormulaArray = '={IF(A2:A100>10, "High", "Low")}'

# Extend the array formula to the whole range
rng.api.FillDown()
```

In the script above, Python first opens an Excel workbook and selects a specific sheet. It then identifies a range where the formula needs to be applied. Following this, Python writes the desired array formula into the first cell of the range using Excel's FormulaArray API. Lastly, the FillDown() method is used to extend the formula to the whole range. A task that could have been quite cumbersome if done manually, is performed in a breeze with Python leading the band.

Advanced Excel formulas are the hidden gems that surface when Python's wand swishes through the crystal sea of Excel. Array formulas, dynamic ranges, boolean logic, nested IFs - are beyond just mere functionalities of Excel. They are potent tools that can catalyze your analytics prowess, turning raw data into polished insights, and challenges into solutions.

Ultimately, by supplementing Excel's inherent abilities with Python's power and flexibility, you can leverage these advanced formulas to perform ever increasingly complex tasks, optimize performance, and unlock new possibilities that render your outputs more valuable, your analyses more profound, and your strategies more influential.

Real-time Data in Excel - Coming up next

Brace for impact as we raise the curtain on another spellbinding act within the grand theatre that is Excel! Prepare to delve into the kinetic cascade effortlessly orchestrated by Python - the symphony of Event-Driven Programming in Excel.

In essence, event-driven programming is the equivalent of a reactive orchestra, awaiting the maestro's nod or the audience's applause to spring into action. It provides a dynamic sequence of actions triggered by various interactions or 'events' within the Excel ecosystem.

Let's discover the various events that Excel recognizes and how Python can drastically simplify the whole process using xlwings and its event handling capabilities.

In xlwings, events are divided into two categories: Workbook events and Worksheet events. Workbook events encompass scenarios like opening a workbook, changing a workbook, etc. Worksheet events include triggering operations when a cell or range is edited.

Consider a scenario where you want to trigger a calculation whenever a specific cell is updated. In Excel, this would involve writing VBA code. However, with Python, it's just a straightforward snippet:

```python
import xlwings as xw

@xw.func(async_mode='threading')
def track_changes():
```

```
app = xw.apps.active

app.sheets['Sheet1'].range('A1').api.Font.ColorIndex = 8   #
Applying certain formatting changes

return app.sheets['Sheet1'].range('A1').value * 2  # Perform
calculation
```
``` ` ` `

Here, Python's decorator `@xw.func(async_mode='threading')` is set up to monitor changes in cell 'A1'. Once a change is detected, a formatting is applied, and Python performs the specified calculation.

Event-driven programming opens the doors to highly responsive, user-friendly interfaces where every mouse-click or keystroke empowers the user, allowing them to weave multiple operations without being lost in the labyrinth of function-calls or procedure executions.

Knitting the threads of event-driven programming into your Excel-land, Python proves an invaluable ally in managing critical operations. Automating processes based on user activity, tracking changes in data, or implementing conditional programming - these are just a few verses of the symphony Python executes within the grand theatre that is Excel.

Now imagine carrying this performance from your workstation to the world-wide web! The next act weaves Python's web of wisdom to sling through real-time data streams and web-related operations in Excel.

With Python as the conductor, we have traversed through
```

the realms of advanced Excel formulas and the cadance of event-driven programming. The versatility and dynamism it breathes into the theatre that is Excel become ever more apparent.

The stage is now set for the next bewitching performance of Python with Excel, dealing with perhaps one of the most challenging yet rewarding score - real-time data. Hold your breath as we are about to dive into a saga where lifeless Excel cells transform into a dynamic organism pulsating with real-time data, all under the maestro's baton - Python.

Complex Data Types and Python Classes

Complex data types in Excel include arrays, tables, and ranges, whose full potential can often remain unexplored due to their inherent complexity. However, here's where Python orchestrates a magnum opus, leveraging its expressive classes to manage and manipulate these complex data types with effortless harmony.

Let's envision a scenario: Suppose you have a table of stock data in Excel, but you want to organize each stock into a Python class with specialized methods, say to calculate moving averages or predict future prices. Creating this class in Python can unlock a higher level of data organization and manipulation:

```python
import pandas as pd

class Stock:
```

```
def __init__(self, dataframe):
    self.data = dataframe
    self.close = dataframe['Close']

def moving_average(self, window):
    return self.close.rolling(window=window).mean()

def predict_prices(self):
    # User-specified prediction logic
    pass
```

Once this class is devised, it can be utilised to manipulate stock data in Excel through Python's Pandora box of versatility. Python classes provide a systematic way of encapsulating and organizing data. When combined with Excel's vast data representation options, the possibilities for data analysis, cleaning, and manipulation are profoundly amplified.

From establishing relationships between different data types, constructing hierarchies for better design, to creating reusable code, Python classes transcend many of the conventional limitations of Excel, driving us towards a highly efficient and effective data management system.

Real-time Data in Excel

Data, in its most fundamental state, is like a river - it constantly moves, ebbs and flows, adapting to the contours of the environment. Like a maestro's baton that controls the orchestra's pace and intensity, real-time data represents the pulse and rhythm of the financial world. Let's now step into the exciting paradigm where we take control of that data within the framework of Excel, directed and orchestrated by the versatile baton of Python.

The dynamic nature of data underscores the need for real-time data analysis — the capability to persistently stay in tune with ongoing changes and trends. Especially in financial analysis, where delay can mean missed opportunities or undue risks, real-time data becomes the heart of decision-making. This is where the power of Python strides confidently into the spotlight, allowing us to introduce real-time data into our Excel worksheets.

Python provides an expansive suite of libraries such as sockets, requests, aiohttp for fetching real-time data from the internet. Moreover, handling streaming data from APIs finds a companion in Python's AsyncIO library, a high-level module to handle and manage asyncio tasks, ensuring you remain on top of dynamic market fluctuations.

Imagine a scenario where you need to perform real-time analysis of stock prices. Through Python and Excel, this becomes effortlessly manageable:

```python
import requests
import pandas as pd
import xlwings as xw

def fetch_live_data(stock_ticker):
    API_URL        =        "https://www.alphavantage.co/query?
function=TIME_SERIES_INTRADAY&symbol={}
```

```
&interval=1min&apikey=YOUR_API_KEY".format(stock_ticke
r)
    response = requests.get(API_URL)
    data = response.json()
    data_frame = pd.DataFrame.from_dict(data['Time Series
(1min)'], orient='index')
    data_frame = data_frame.apply(pd.to_numeric)

    return data_frame

ticker = "AAPL"
stock_data = fetch_live_data(ticker)
stock_data["4. close"].plot() # plotting real-time graph

# Live update in Excel
xw.view(stock_data)
` ` `
```

By running this script throughout the trading day, your Excel workbook updates in real time, providing the latest market data at your fingertips.

Yet, planting the seed of real-time data into the fertile ground of Excel is just the beginning. With this newfound strength, one can now automate the execution of strategic decisions based on real-time insights, confidently navigating the ebb and flow of market dynamics.

Using Excel as a Front-end Interface

The call of our narrative has led us to an exciting realm

of Python-Excel symbiosis, wherein Excel evolves beyond a mere spreadsheet application. It's here that Excel dons a new role - that of a powerful front-end interface, acting as a conduit between the computational prowess of Python and the decision-making framework that drives your financial world. Let's begin, then, this undeniably fascinating symphony where Python and Excel create an interactive harmony.

When it comes to interactiveness and accessibility, Excel as a user-interface is a reliable choice. Its grid structure provides a practical canvas for organizing and displaying data, whilst the power of Python broadens Excel's horizon, enabling an array of functionalities limited only by one's imagination. Let's dive into the world of forms, event-driven programming, and custom functions.

Consider a scenario of financial forecasting interface designed within Excel. Excel acts as the front-end - a locus for user inputs and output display, while Python serves as the back-end, processing data and performing the computational heavy lifting.

```python
import xlwings as xw
from sklearn.linear_model import LinearRegression

def forecast_data():
    # Connecting the interface
    wb = xw.Book.caller()
    sheet = wb.sheets['Data']

    # Fetch data
```

```python
    data_range = sheet.range('A1').expand()
    data_values       =       data_range.options(pd.DataFrame,
index=False, header=True).value

    # Predictive Modeling
    model = LinearRegression()
    model.fit(data_values[['Input1',                    'Input2']],
data_values['Output'])

    # Form Controls for Predictive Inputs
    input_values = sheet.range('G3:G4').value

    # Forecast
    forecast = model.predict([input_values])

    # Output to Excel Interface
    sheet.range('H4').value = forecast[0]

@xw.func
@xw.arg('trigger', trigger=True)
def on_guess_button_clicked(trigger):
    if trigger:
        forecast_data()
` ` `
```

In this script, Excel fields serve to collect user inputs, with Python-modelled forecast reflected back to Excel. It's an impeccable manipulation, where the Excel worksheet, traditionally stationary, is now a dynamic and participatory interface, transforming your clarity and efficiency in financial forecasting endeavors.

The narrative above epitomizes the prowess of Excel as a front-end interface, an undeniably disruptive force wielded by Python. Tag-teamed with Python, Excel is no longer a simple spreadsheet tool. Instead, it grows into a full-stack application, providing the 'one-two punch,' a combination of a user-friendly interface and deep computational strength.

In the closing chapter of this section, we recognize the extraordinary transformation of Excel under the stewardship of Python. It's a metamorphosis from a static spreadsheet into a dynamic user-interface that complements your business and financial analytics needs. It places data processing and decision-making capabilities directly into the hands of the user, paving the way for interactive, real-time financial analyses.

CHAPTER 5:
STATISTICAL
ANALYSIS AND
FINANCIAL
MODELING WITH
PYTHON AND EXCEL

Exploratory Data Analysis

Diving deeper into the heart of Python's prowess, let's tune into the rhythm of Exploratory Data Analysis, often abbreviated as EDA. This important symphony in our Python-for-Excel sonata serves an undeniable purpose, revealing the patterns, anomalies, hypotheses, and structures of our data. Its tantalising rhythm confirms Python's utility and myriad applications in financial analytics. Journey with me, then, on this data exploration trail, unveiling the hidden symmetries of our financial universe.

Exploratory Data Analysis, in the nirvana of Python and Excel duet, serves as the high ground, enabling us to observe the landscape of our data terrain from a strategic vantage point.

Riding on Python's shoulder, we traverse through magnificent valleys of data insights, shedding refreshing light onto Excel's vast datasets.

The core essence of EDA lies in diving deep to comprehend our data's characteristics and inner structure. Python extends its analytical prowess for this quest, equipping us with statistical and visualisation libraries like matplotlib, seaborn, pandas, and more. These tools harmonize with Excel's structure, offering insights into our data and unravelling strategic paths for further data processing.

Consider an Excel sheet, densely populated with the financial data of a series of stock prices. The exercise of exploratory data analysis would involve multiple stages, starting with a determination of basic descriptors.

```python
import pandas as pd

# Import data from Excel into a pandas DataFrame
df = pd.read_excel('FinancialData.xlsx')

# Generate descriptive statistics of the DataFrame
stats = df.describe()
```

The code above towing with it a summary of mean, median, standard deviation, minimum, quartiles, and maximum values, forging a potent snapshot of our data's distribution.

Further, the creation of visualisations, such as a histogram, can be a potent tool to intuitively understand your data.

```python
import matplotlib.pyplot as plt

# Plot histogram of a specific stock's historical prices
plt.hist(df['StockPrice'], bins=30, edgecolor='black')
plt.title('Stock Price Distribution')
plt.xlabel('Price')
plt.ylabel('Frequency')
plt.show()
```

This script breathes life into our data, sculpting an insightful histogram that allows us to interpret the stock prices' distribution. It also offers a window to anomalies and spikes, a tantalising glimpse into potential risks and opportunities.

In the landscape of Python and Excel, EDA vindicates the rhythm of data exploration, invoking curiosity and transparency. It leads us into the innermost chasms of our data, offering insights into the underlying structure, feeding our financial intellect, and guiding our next steps. Armed with EDA, we can enhance our understanding, ensuring our investments strike the right chord in the grand ensemble of financial markets.

Financial Modeling and Forecasting

Take a breath and let the breeze guide your ship. It's time we crossed the Rubicon, venturing from EDA's shores to the thrilling tempest of financial modeling and forecasting.

Together, let's navigate this potent blend of Python's precision and Excel's intimacy. Stand steady, for the winds of prediction are laden with the enchantment of algebra, the siren call of data manipulation, and the powerful gusts of machine learning.

In this dynamic tangle of numbers, our first stop is financial modeling. At its core, financial modeling is a scalpel - it dissects financial data, isolating components that can provide intriguing insights or trends. These models, powered by Python's prowess and Excel's versatility, optimize our financial data structures and algorithms, transforming raw financial data into strategic intelligence.

Consider, for example, a fundamental financial model – the ominous sounding 'Discounted Cash Flow' or DCF model. Deploying Python's high-fidelity calculations and Excel's user-friendly interface, it becomes a classical symphony. By projecting future cash flows and discounting them to their present value, the DCF gives us a metric to evaluate investment opportunities.

```python
import numpy as np

# Projected future cash flows for next five years
cash_flows = np.array([50000, 55000, 60000, 65000, 70000])

# Discount rate
rate = 0.05

# Discounted cash flows
dcf = np.sum(cash_flows / (1 + rate)**np.arange(1, 6))
```

```
` ` `
```

This small snippet of code nests the power of Python within the DCF model, spawning a powerful decision-making tool.

Next, we voyage to uncharted waters: financial forecasting. With the rhythmic pounding of data-driven algorithms, forecasting reads the tea leaves of past and present data to divine future financial trends. When imbued with Python's capabilities - the likes of Time Series Forecasting, ARIMA, and LSTM models - the abstract canvas of Excel datasets turns into vibrant murals of predictive analysis.

Let's consider a simplified forecasting scenario involving time-series data (financial time series, to be precise) and an ARIMA model.

```python
from statsmodels.tsa.arima_model import ARIMA

# Fit an ARIMA(5,1,0) model to the financial time series
model = ARIMA(df['FinancialColumn'], order=(5,1,0))
model_fit = model.fit(disp=0)

# Generate future predictions
forecast = model_fit.forecast(steps=10)
```

Python's ARIMA model, coupled with Excel's structured financial data, generates a prediction of our chosen metric's future values. It's akin to having your telescope on a clear night in the open ocean: the future's constellation gleams with captivating insights.

In essence, Financial Modeling and Forecasting's marriage to Python and Excel illuminates the night sky of the financial universe. Mundane financial data shed their earthly shells, metamorphosing into starry insights and navigational guides. Imperative to financial decision-making, they set the course for investment strategies, marking out safe harbours and treacherous storms. Their symphony resonates across the ocean of financial data, harmonising the cacophonous data into tuneful wisdom. In its lyrics, we find our financial journey's rhythm.

In the realm of Python and Excel, modeling, and forecasting weave predictive tapestries from abstract strands of data. As experienced sailors of this algorithmic sea, we now carry in our hands the compass of strategic decision-making. Yet, the melody of this Python-Excel concert is far from completed. Our next voyage awaits - starring statistical tests and the mariner's star of Python libraries, they call forth the uncovering of regression analysis. Emerging from the mists of uncertainty, it promises to carry our financial sagas into the land of strategic decision-making.

Regression Analysis

In the expansive domain of financial analysis, Regression Analysis is like a wise old sage living among the mystic analytics mountains, known for his reputation of unravelling the complexities of relationships between variables. The sage uses the mathematical wand of regression models, where independent variables' effects on dependent variables are ingeniously quantified for predictions and forecasting. The language the sage talks in is a sleek blend of

Python's syntax and Excel's arithmetic grandeur.

To perceive the gravity of regression analysis, let's translate theory into action with the simplest form of it: Simple Linear Regression. Picture a scenario in a financial context where, as an analyst, you are curious about finding if a relationship exists between a company's advertising spends (independent variable) and its sales generated (dependent variable).

```python
import pandas as pd
from sklearn.linear_model import LinearRegression

# Load the dataset into pandas DataFrame
df = pd.read_excel('financial_data.xlsx')

# Define predictors and target variable
X = df[['Advertising']]
y = df['Sales']

# Instantiate and fit the model
model = LinearRegression()
model.fit(X, y)
```

Brief yet potent, this example exhibits Python working its magic on Excel data to perform Simple Linear Regression. The model's trained weights can later be used to predict the sales from advertising spends.

But the layers of complexity are far from being fully unfolded.

In the enchanting world of regression lies another more robust method: Multiple Linear Regression. As the name suggests, this form of regression lets you inspect the impact of multiple independent variables on a dependent variable.

```python
# Define multiple predictors and target variable
X = df[['Advertising', 'Marketing', 'ProductQuality']]
y = df['Sales']

# Instantiate and fit the model
model = LinearRegression()
model.fit(X, y)
```

Unfolding Python's power makes it easy to extend the methodology to include more number of predictors, thereby being able to predict sales not just based on advertising spends, but also incorporating factors such as marketing budget and product quality.

In its essence, regression analysis is the chronicle of relationships. It mutates the nebulous concepts into tangible facets with defined magnitudes and directions. Over the backdrop of financial analysis, regression analysis becomes a lens, focusing the raw light of data into illuminating insights. In the realm of correlations and causations, it serves as a compass, orientating one towards gaining predictive insights and associative inferences.

Hypothesis Testing

Hypothesis Testing, in its quintessence, is a statistical detective, probing through data to either validate or disprove an assumption about it. Be it verifying theories about market operations or authenticating financial models, Hypothesis Testing works as an analytical touchstone to expose factual facets from deceptive mirages.

A fundamental tool in the arsenal of Hypothesis Testing is the p-value, a statistical barometer that measures the likelihood of our data, given the validity of a proposed hypothesis. A smaller p-value indicates the hypothesis is less likely to be true, while a larger one implies soundness of our theoretical supposition.

To weave this high-powered process with Python and Excel, let's study an exemplary scenario. As a financial analyst, you may want to test the average return of a stock over a stipulated period. The null hypothesis (H0) in this case may be that the mean return is zero. A Python integration with Excel to perform this test would look like this:

```python
from scipy import stats

# Load the data into pandas DataFrame
df = pd.read_excel('stock_returns.xlsx')

# compute the test statistic and p-value
test_statistic, p_value = stats.ttest_1samp(df['Return'], 0)

print(f"Test Statistic: {test_statistic}\nP-value: {p_value}")
```

In this code block, we use the SciPy library's \`ttest_1samp \` function to perform a one-sample t-test on the stock returns loaded from an Excel spreadsheet. If the p-value is less than your threshold (like 0.05), you might reject the null hypothesis and conclude that the average return is statistically significantly different from zero.

Multi-faceted as it is, Hypothesis Testing unfolds various other methods like Chi-Square tests, ANOVA, etc., ready to be woven into Python, reinforcing our control over Excel data.

Drinking deep from the font of Hypothesis Testing, we emerge refreshingly enlightened, navigating the course of data with renewed confidence. It empowers us as analysis explorers, bolstering our conviction against conjecture, armed with the statistical rigour of Python and Excel. The statistical lens has now sharper focus, ready to dissect data with enhanced precision.

Monte Carlo Simulations

Monte Carlo Simulations, named after the renowned gambling hotspot in Monaco, elegantly ushers in the concepts of randomness and probabilities to mimic real-world systems. These simulated repetitions of random variables, running into thousands of iterations, unfurl a realm of potential outcomes. This provides an anthology of "what-if" scenarios to predict and strategize where traditional deterministic models may fail.

Visualize it as running identical twins of a reality where variegated outcomes unfurl influenced by the intrinsic squirrelly nature of probabilities. The results? A panorama of potential outcomes, dispersing in different directions, offering a profound perspective into risk management and decision-making.

For instance, consider an Excel spreadsheet containing years of monthly returns on a particular asset. We could conduct a Monte Carlo simulation to forecast how those returns might look for the following year. The Python code integrated into Excel to accomplish this task might look something like:

```python
import numpy as np

# Load the data into pandas DataFrame
df = pd.read_excel('monthly_returns.xlsx')

# compute mean and standard deviation
mean_return = df['Return'].mean()
std_return = df['Return'].std()

# Run Monte Carlo simulation
simulated_returns   =   np.random.normal(mean_return, std_return, 12)

print("Simulated Returns:")
print(simulated_returns)
```

This simulation takes monthly return data and uses it to create a hypothetical set of twelve monthly returns for the next year, using the normal distribution as a model of randomness. This is but a glimpse of the intricate possibilities Monte Carlo Simulations open for effective planning and enhanced decision-making.

With the Monte Carlo lessons etched in our minds, we stand at the edge of the statistical horizon, armed for the world of uncertainties. Excel's grandeur with the Python integration forms the compass, navigating through the financial oceans' unpredictability. The learned techniques, be it the predictive prowess of Regression Analysis, the validating authority of Hypothesis Testing or the apt adaptation of Monte Carlo Simulations, our navigation is precise and confident. Now, let us set our sails towards uncharted financial waters as we delve deeper into Time-Series Analysis in the subsequent chapter. Onwards, to the next adventure!

Portfolio Optimization

Portfolio Optimization finds its roots within Modern Portfolio Theory (MPT), a theory unearthing the balance between risk and return within an investment portfolio. At the core of MPT stands the "Efficient Frontier"- a beacon, guiding investors through the darkness of risk towards the shores of optimal returns.

So, what's this got to do with Python and Excel? Well, Python's robust mathematical frameworks and Excel's accessible financial tools come together in high fidelity to transpose the theoretical models of MPT into practical, actionable investment strategies. By working in tandem, they transform Excel from a static analytical tool into a dynamic portfolio optimization workshop.

For illustration, we could construct a portfolio of three assets-stocks from Apple, Microsoft, and Tesla. We'll employ Python within Excel to simulate thousands of potential portfolio allocations. By using Excel's built-in statistical functions alongside Python's robust libraries, we can calculate the expected returns and risks for each potential allocation and determine an optimal balance.

```python
import pandas as pd
import numpy as np
from scipy.optimize import minimize

# Load historical price data into pandas DataFrames
apple = pd.read_excel('apple.xlsx')
microsoft = pd.read_excel('microsoft.xlsx')
tesla = pd.read_excel('tesla.xlsx')

# Merge on dates and calculate log returns
prices = pd.concat([apple, microsoft, tesla], axis=1, join='inner')
log_returns = np.log(prices / prices.shift(1))

# Define the objective function (negative Sharpe Ratio)
def objective(weights):
    return -np.mean(log_returns @ weights) / np.std(log_returns @ weights)

# Initial guess equal weights
init_guess = np.repeat(1/prices.shape[1], prices.shape[1])
# All weights must sum to 1
constraints = ({'type': 'eq', 'fun': lambda x: np.sum(x) - 1})
results      =      minimize(objective,      init_guess,
```

```
constraints=constraints)
optimal_weights = results.x

print("Optimal Portfolio Weights:")
print(optimal_weights)
```

This simulation evaluates countless combinations of allocations to each of the three stocks, aiming to generate the best returns relative to the level of risk, utilizing the Sharpe Ratio as its guiding light. The output provides the optimal weights for each stock in your portfolio to achieve maximum portfolio performance.

CHAPTER 6:
INTEGRATING PYTHON MACHINE LEARNING WITH EXCEL

Introduction to Machine Learning

Drawing inspiration from the profound lessons of Portfolio Optimization, we now raise our anchor to venture into the mystic realm of Machine Learning. This intriguing expanse conjoins the worlds of computational science and finance, revolving around the axis of Python and Excel. An echo from the depths of technology meets the resonating notes of financial intelligence, choreographing an elegant dance of logical relations and dynamic inference. Shield yourself in the armour of anticipation, for we are stepping into the promising frontiers of Machine Learning, where the encounter with the unexpected becomes an essential part of our journey.

Machine Learning, a cornerstone of Artificial Intelligence, is the technology of enabling machines to learn from data, understand patterns, make decisions, and improve over time without being explicitly programmed to do so. At the heart of it lie algorithms that feed on data, digest and learn from them, and then apply their learning to make informed predictions or decisions.

So how does this tie into our theme? In the arena of finance, Machine Learning equips us with the gauntlet to seize not just evident data patterns but also subtle, hidden correlations. Excel lays the foundation, cleansing and presenting data for consumption, while Python, with its rich bounty of Machine Learning libraries like scikit-learn and TensorFlow, makes model building and data interpretation a reality.

Let's consider analysing financial markets with Excel and Python. Machine Learning can aid in predictive analytics, forecasting future prices of financial assets, and identifying investment opportunities based on past trends and various indicators. Python, with its wide range of Machine Learning libraries, dramatically simplifies this task. Here is a simple example of a regression model predicting stock prices:

```python
import pandas as pd
from sklearn.model_selection import train_test_split
from sklearn.linear_model import LinearRegression

# Load the data
data = pd.read_excel('stock_data.xlsx')

# Select features and target
features = data[['Open', 'High', 'Low', 'Volume']]
target = data['Close']
```

```
# Split into training and test datasets
X_train, X_test, y_train, y_test = train_test_split(features,
target, test_size=0.2, random_state=0)

# Create a linear regression model
model = LinearRegression()

# fit our model with our training data
model.fit(X_train, y_train)

# Predict closing prices using our test dataset
predictions = model.predict(X_test)
```
` ` `

This example uses the LinearRegression model from the scikit-learn library in Python to predict the closing price of a stock based on its opening price, high, low, and volume.

Predictive Modeling

Here, we navigate the territories where statistical techniques and AI intersect to predict outcomes. The crossroads where our decisions, influenced by projections of the future, seek to shatter the glass ceilings set by the past. This chapter is an invitation to explore predictive modeling - a voyage through the ebbs and flows of Excel's organized data, steered by Python's powerful forecasting abilities.

Predictive Modeling employs statistical methods and machine learning algorithms to predict future outcomes based on historical data. The task can be as simple as predicting sales trends for the next quarter, or as complex as forecasting stock prices utilizing a bewildering array of variables.

To successfully deploy Predictive Modeling with Python in the realm of Excel, we need a mathematician's analytical prowess, a programmer's love for logical patterns, and a seasoned traveller's curiosity to discern previously overlooked paths.

Let's dig into an illustration using Python and Excel for predictive modeling in finance. Suppose we have a dataset containing historical daily closing prices of a particular stock:

```python
import pandas as pd
from sklearn.model_selection import train_test_split
from sklearn.linear_model import LinearRegression

# Import Excel file and convert to DataFrame
df = pd.read_excel("stock_data.xlsx")

# Extract 'Close Price' series and transform data into array
close_price = df['Close'].values.reshape(-1,1)

# Generate series of consecutive numbers to represent 'Days'
days = pd.Series(range(1,len(df)+1)).values.reshape(-1,1)

# Split the data into train and test datasets
X_train, X_test, y_train, y_test = train_test_split(days, close_price, test_size=0.25, random_state=0)

# Apply Linear Regression to the dataset
```

```
model = LinearRegression()
model.fit(X_train, y_train)

# Predict 'Close Price' for the test dataset
predicted_prices = model.predict(X_test)
` ` `
```

In the above example, the Linear Regression Model uses the 'Days' as a predictor of 'Close Price'. The result is a set of future closing price forecasts, fuelled by the historical data.

Glimpses of Tomorrow: The Echoes of Predictive Modeling

Predictive Modeling requires a fine balance of knowledge, intuition, and innovativeness. But when done right, it can unlock new realms of possibilities, turning potential into reality. In its truest essence, Predictive Modeling is sailing into the future, guided by the lessons from the crossroads of history - a journey embarking from the shores of what was, to the horizon of what could be.

Peering into the realm of predictive modeling through the lens of Python and Excel, we find our reflection in a world moulded by data and algorithms, where, inspired by the past, we strive to sketch the outlines of the future. The systematic arts of forecasting pave the path ahead, bringing clarity to the murky waters of uncertainty. Thus, instilled with newfound wisdom, let us immerse ourselves into the flowing currents of the chapters that lie ahead, ready to dive deeper into the symbiosis between Python, Excel, and the universe of data-driven finance.

Classification Algorithms

On the grand canvas that is the universe of data, patterns form abstract arrangements waiting to be deciphered. Shadows of trends reel in shimmers of insight, altering the spectrum of our comprehension. Within this tableau of understanding, Classification Algorithms emerge as crucial authorities profoundly shaping our exploration.

Built atop the strong pillars of Python's programming prowess and Excel's data structuring adeptness, these algorithms instill a sense of ordered clarity to the otherwise chaotic landscape of data. They serve as the unseen binding force, identifying patterns and segregating data into distinct categories or 'classes'. With them, we discover a new dimension of spatiality in the otherwise flat plane of Excel spreadsheets—a facet where each entry, each cell, aligns to a distinctive identity.

Classification Algorithms, in the grand scheme of machine learning, are the algorithms responsible for categorizing data into specified classes. Depending on the nature of the problem, these classifications can be binary (Yes or No, True or False) or multiclass (Categorizing a news article into 'Sports', 'Entertainment', 'Politics', etc.).

To trace the steps along this labyrinth of classification, let's create a simple example in Python and Excel where we use the Logistic Regression algorithm—a common linear classifier —to identify whether a loan applicant would be able to repay their loan or default on it. Assume we have a spreadsheet that consists of applicant data, including their 'Income', 'Credit Score', and a 'Defaulted' column which marks whether the applicant defaulted on their previous loan.

```python
import pandas as pd
from sklearn.model_selection import train_test_split
from sklearn.linear_model import LogisticRegression

# Import Excel file and convert to DataFrame
df = pd.read_excel("loan_data.xlsx")

# Create feature and target datasets
feature_cols = ['Income', 'Credit_score']
X = df[feature_cols]
y = df['Defaulted']

# Split the data into train and test datasets
X_train, X_test, y_train, y_test = train_test_split(X, y, test_size=0.25, random_state=0)

# Apply Logistic Regression to the dataset
clf = LogisticRegression()
clf.fit(X_train, y_train)

# Predict 'Defaulted' for the test dataset
predicted_default = clf.predict(X_test)
```

In this Python example, 'Income' and 'Credit Score' are the predictors, used to classify whether an applicant is likely to 'Default' on their loan or not.

Decoding Complexity: The Symphony of Classification

Algorithms

When we delve into the artful discipline of Classification Algorithms, we immerse ourselves in a realm where Python's advanced mathematical libraries converge with the structured sophistication of Excel data matrices. Here, the abstract vowel sounds of patterns transgress into the consonants of comprehension, shaping the narrative of understanding.

These algorithms are not mere tools; they parallel the multifaceted hues of an artist's palette—each color, each algorithm, capable of blending with others to expand the breadth of insights to unforeseen dimensions. Their symphony opens the avenues of future chapters, leading us on a journey to master the disciplined performance of machine learning.

Regression Algorithms

Steeped in the precision of mathematical constructs and the dexterity of Python's programming, Regression Algorithms offer us a way to predict a continuous target variable based on one or more feature variables. This quantum leap from classification predictions transcends the simplicity of discrete categories, introducing us to the captivating realm of forecasts represented on continuous spectrums.

Regression Algorithms in machine learning are the mathematical models that enable us to predict a continuous output based on the relationship between variables. If Classification Algorithms are the compass that help us navigate the categorical map of data, then Regression Algorithms are the ship that lets us sail the unfathomable oceans of continuous data.

In the vast sea of regression schemes, one 'ship' that stands tall is the Linear Regression Algorithm. This algorithm is fundamental to regression prediction. It predicts a dependent variable value (y) based on a given independent variable (x). So, it finds the line of fit to a given data set.

Suppose we have a dataset, which comprises the 'Monthly Income(in $)' and 'Monthly Spendings(in $)'. To predict 'Monthly Spendings' based on 'Monthly Income,' we can employ the Linear Regression model as illustrated below.

```python
import pandas as pd
from sklearn.model_selection import train_test_split
from sklearn.linear_model import LinearRegression

# Import data from Excel file and convert to DataFrame
df = pd.read_excel("income_spendings_data.xlsx")

# Define feature and target datasets
feature_col = ['Monthly_Income']
X = df[feature_col]
y = df['Monthly_Spendings']

# Create training and test datasets
X_train, X_test, y_train, y_test = train_test_split(X, y, test_size=0.2, random_state=0)

# Apply Linear Regression to the dataset
regressor = LinearRegression()
```

```
regressor.fit(X_train, y_train)

# Forecast 'Monthly_Spendings' for the test dataset
predicted_spendings = regressor.predict(X_test)
```

This example elucidates how we can use Python and Excel together for predictive modelling in finance, exploring the relationship between 'Monthly Income' and 'Monthly Spendings'.

Clustering Algorithms

We stand at the doorway to an entirely new perspective on interpreting the symphony of numbers. As we bid farewell to regression, the attention shifts to a fresh narrative - Clustering Algorithms. Like an archaeologist chiseling away at ancient stone, we too prepare to reveal the obscured patterns and take a deep dive into the realm of unsupervised learning.

Unlike regression's guided approach, clustering follows the exploratory path—it uncovers from disorder the hidden patterns, and presents a map to navigate data without predefined targets. Its predictions, unlike the serenity of a placid lake, shake the confines of a rigid box, liberating us into the boundless world of Python-powered Excel analytics.

The realm of Clustering Algorithms is a landscape of diverse and innovative techniques that are shapeshifters, adept in carving out natural associations and clusters out of seemingly chaotic datasets. K-Means and Hierarchical clustering are two such prominent techniques.

Imagine, you are a financial analyst with a hefty financial dataset and you're tasked with identifying the distinct styles of investment among your company's client base. Each client's investment style is a spectral blend of hundreds of transactions, forming a rich repository of information. By using Python's exceptional libraries and Excel's versatile interface, we can analyze this intricate dataset in the wink of an eye.

Take for instance, the K-Means Clustering algorithm. It essentially groups your clients into 'k' number of clusters, where each client belongs to the cluster with the nearest mean investment style. Code for such an algorithm might begin as follows:

```python
from sklearn.cluster import KMeans
import pandas as pd

# Data loading from Excel to DataFrame
df = pd.read_excel("clients_investment_data.xlsx")

# Selecting feature columns
features_cols = ['Investment_A', 'Investment_B', 'Investment_C']
X = df[features_cols]

# Apply K-Means Clustering
kmeans = KMeans(n_clusters=3)
kmeans.fit(X)
```

```
# Adding the cluster labels to the DataFrame
df['investment_style_cluster'] = kmeans.labels_

df.to_excel('clustered_investment_data.xlsx')
```

This example simplifies how Python's K-Means Clustering can be harnessed within Excel to indicate clear investment style patterns among clients in a large financial dataset.

Unseen patterns come to life under the discerning eye of the clustering algorithms. They energetically dissect the muddy rivers of unlabelled data, revealing the vibrant ecosystem within. The elegance of clustering lies in its ability to generate insights without guided instruction, making it the perfect tool when working with unlabelled datasets— a common occurrence in the world of data analytics.

In the heart of clustering lies the aspiration to identify patterns obscured by the proximity of numbers and figures - to partition the datasets and group them into meaningful clusters based on identified similarities.

Paired with Python's versatility and thrust into Excel's familiar environment, clustering algorithms tell a tale of patterns, whispers of similarities, and echoes of correlations. As they meticulously partition and group datasets to unveil unseen stories, a symphony of order emerges from the tedious disarray of complex data.

Anomaly Detection

In the world of numbers that typically resonate with patterns and clusters, the concept of anomaly detection pushes your understanding to embrace the errant. Through this chapter, we aim to echo the potent belief - that understanding deviations, not just conformities, unlock an entirely new vista of comprehension in data analysis.

Anomalies, simply put, are data points that deviate significantly from the regular trends or patterns in your dataset. The finance landscape is rich with contexts where anomaly detection comes into play - be it identifying fraudulent card transactions, unexpected market shifts, losses due to unusual activities, or any significant variance that could imply an actionable insight.

Mastering the art of Anomaly Detection is crafting a sentinel that never sleeps. With Python and Excel, we can design algorithms that meticulously pick out these unusual patterns from a sea of data in seemingly real-time.

To put this into perspective with a practical example, consider a scenario where we have transaction data of a financial institution and we aim to identify possible fraud. Python and Excel combine seamlessly to enable this.

Here's where an outlier detection algorithm package named Scikit-Learn comes to play. Scikit-Learn's Local Outlier Factor(LOF) can come in handy for this purpose. This code snippet shows how:

```python
from sklearn.neighbors import LocalOutlierFactor
```

```
import pandas as pd

# Load transaction data from Excel to DataFrame
df = pd.read_excel("transaction_data.xlsx")

# Features for the LOF algorithm
feature_cols = ['Amount', 'TransactionType', 'Location']
X = df[feature_cols]

# Apply LOF
lof = LocalOutlierFactor(n_neighbors=20, contamination=0.1)
df['Outlier'] = lof.fit_predict(X)

# Save the data with flagged outliers back to Excel
df.to_excel('flagged_outliers_transaction_data.xlsx')
```

In this example output, the `Outlier` column will have a value of -1 for transactions the LOF algorithm determines as outliers, i.e., potential fraud transactions.

Anomaly detection is your very own eureka moment in the boundless mine of data analytics. It gives you the power to discover the undiscovered, to question the status quo, and to spot the unforeseen. In the chaos of numbers, anomaly detection is your path to finding the silent outliers that often hold the loudest tales.

The incessant chatter of the financial world deciphers into discernible patterns and predictable clusters with the power vested by anomaly detection. And the amalgamation of Python's versatile capabilities and Excel's intuitive interface paves this path of serendipitous discovery where every anomaly potentially offers a game-changing insight for firms.

The world of finance is enriched with the use of anomaly detection. The outliers in data become the drivers of change, pointing to critical insights and opportunities. As we walk you through the distinct territories of detection algorithms, understand that each algorithm is an individual lens through which you view the world of data.

With Python's extensive libraries and Excel's powerful suite of tools, data doesn't just speak; it sings, murmurs, and sometimes shouts out patterns and anomalies, each echo ushering another discovery.

Model Evaluation and Validation

To appreciate the essence of model evaluation and validation, it's pivotal to understand its need in the first place. After training a model, we need to ascertain its performance metric, i.e., how well it works with new, unseen data. The goal of a good model should be to generalise well, not just fitting the training data.

The process encompasses two key segments - 'validation,' which determines how well the model has understood the nuances of the training data, and 'evaluation,' through which the model's performance with new data gets assayed. This process helps us nullify the risk of overfitting the data, where the model is too intricately linked with the training data and fails to handle new data efficiently.

Python lends a hand to facilitate this process. Scikit-Learn, one of Python's opensource libraries, comes stocked with plentiful functions for model evaluation and validation. Sklearn.metrics, for instance, provides numerous methods to calculate different types of evaluation metrics such as accuracy, precision, recall, and others. Here, let's use it for confusion matrix and classification report:

```python
from sklearn.metrics import confusion_matrix, classification_report
import pandas as pd

# Load validated output data from Excel to DataFrame
df = pd.read_excel("validated_output_data.xlsx")

# Generate confusion matrix and classification report
y_true = df['TrueLabels']
y_pred = df['PredictedLabels']
conf_mat = confusion_matrix(y_true, y_pred)
print("Confusion Matrix:\n", conf_mat)

class_report = classification_report(y_true, y_pred)
print("Classification Report:\n", class_report)

# Save the reports back to Excel
df_report = pd.DataFrame([str(conf_mat), str(class_report)], columns=['Report'])
df_report.to_excel('evaluation_report.xlsx')
```

In this code, a confusion matrix and a classification report gets generated to gauge the performance of our predictive model. The TrueLabels column represents the correct labels, and the PredictedLabels column denotes the labels predicted by our trained model.

In your journey to build prediction prowess with Python and Excel, model evaluation and validation is the point where you gear up for the final showdown. Every model is just a curious hypothesis until validated and found sturdy. A correctly validated model is like an open book with answers waiting to be deciphered, guiding your machine learning endeavours in the right pathway.

Moreover, proper model validation and evaluation are like the resolution of a captivating plot, the point where a narrative, having traversed through the entanglements of regression algorithms, clustering, and anomaly detection, uncovers the potency of its climax.

Boasting a validated model allows you a glance at a crystal ball, forecasting the future and generating actionable insights. Harnessing the power of Python inside Excel, you can rigorously test your models, understand their strengths and weaknesses, and choose the best one that suits your requirements.

The finely executed art of model evaluation and validation leads to precision, credibility, and scalability. In the end, it becomes the yardstick by which both a model's performance and its potential utility in the real-world scenarios can be equated - the ultimate verdict on its robustness.

Bear in mind that the spotlight on understanding and interpreting model validation and evaluation emanates from its role in ensuring that your hard work in data pre-processing, engineering features, and training the model doesn't go in vain. Now you know that the intricate tapestry woven by the algorithm has its threads in the right place.

We've come a long way, from the humble beginnings of Python and Excel integration to model evaluation and validation. As we draw the curtains on this chapter, remember that our journey of learning and growth is not coming to a halt but is merely changing its course. There's always another chapter, another opportunity, another challenge awaiting at the turn of the page. Let us continue to push the boundaries, innovate, and make a tangible impact. Let's keep turning those pages.

CHAPTER 7: ADVANCED VISUALIZATIONS AND REPORTING WITH PYTHON AND EXCEL

Creating Interactive Dashboards

In the grand epic of data interpretation and understanding, the ability to create interactive dashboards is akin to painting a masterpiece on a blank canvas. It is here that your hard work in manipulating and analyzing data finally emerges in vibrant colors, telling a tale that captures the audience's minds and hearts. So, buckle up as we delve into crafting interactive dashboards, the finesse that turns raw data into fluent dialogue.

Building interactive dashboards is an art, and with Python and Excel acting as our brushes and colors, we are poised to craft compelling data tales. Let this part of our journey offer you an insight into the multidimensionality and multifunctionality embedded within the frameworks of Python and Excel as we tackle the world of interactive dashboards.

Interactive dashboards are potent tools in bridging the gap between raw data and strategic decisions churned out from its analysis. They provide real-time updates, flexible views into the dataset, and engagement aspects that turn the dull numbers into an interactive story. Your data begins a refreshing dialogue with the user, offering insights that static reports often fall short of giving.

Python, being the versatile programming language that it is, offers multiple libraries like Dash, Plotly, and Bokeh for creating visually appealing and interactive dashboards. Combined with Excel's simplicity and widely familiar interface, we can create elaborate dashboards right inside Excel using Python. Let's take a glimpse into how it works:

```python
import pandas as pd
import plotly.express as px

# Load your data from Excel to DataFrame
df = pd.read_excel("your_data_file.xlsx")

# Create an interactive scatter plot with Plotly
fig = px.scatter(df, x="Column1", y="Column2", color="Column3",
        size='Column4', hover_data=['Column5'])

fig.write_html("Interactive_Dashboard.html")
```

Here, we're loading data from an Excel file into a Pandas

DataFrame, then using the Plotly Express library (px) for creating an interactive scatter plot. The final dashboard is saved as an HTML file, which can be embedded into Excel using VBA or opened in any web browser for a standalone interactive dashboard.

The thrilling ride of crafting interactive dashboards highlights the magic that unfolds when Python, an undeniable force in the programming world, teams up with Excel, the long-ruling monarch of spreadsheet applications. This superb duo transforms the somewhat mundane task of interpreting data into an adventure of discovery using interactive dashboards.

Creating these dashboards is not just a mere process; it's unveiling the dynamic tapestry woven with complex data threads, letting vivid patterns of insights surface. It turns the silent chatter of numbers into a vociferous dialogue with the audience, where data no longer remains an enigma but converses, narrates, and facilitates informed decision-making.

The power of interactive dashboards extends beyond just aesthetic appeal—it allows for quick data analysis and fosters a deeper understanding of data from different viewpoints. Excel, with its user-friendly interface, combined with Python, brings about an inherent flexibility allowing users from differing backgrounds to use it effectively.

Generating Professional Reports

If interactive dashboards were a symphony of visual storytelling, consider professional reports as the encore that follows. It complements the enchanting melodies of eye-catching dashboards with harmonizing notes of in-depth insights and professional presentation.

Python and Excel together not only make beautiful music but this duo can deliver awe-inspiring performances in the world of data analysis and professional reporting. Now, let's switch gears and understand the monumental role Python plays when leveraged with Excel to generate professional-grade reports.

Professional reports form the backbone of data-driven decision making in any business environment. They offer a polished, organized, and in-depth view of data analysis, statistics, findings, and recommendations. Enhancing this process with the capabilities of Python takes Excel reporting to new heights, adding unprecedented speed, efficiency, and customization.

The flexibility of Python and its extensive set of libraries provide tools to manipulate data, conduct complex computations, visualize data effectively, and generate sophisticated reports. Best of all, it's scalable for both small and large datasets.

Here's a taste of how it works:

```python
import pandas as pd

# Load your data from Excel to DataFrame
df = pd.read_excel("your_data_file.xlsx")

# Conduct your data analysis...
## ...your beautiful and efficient Python code goes here...
```

```
# Save the results back to Excel
df.to_excel("your_processed_data_file.xlsx")

` ` `
```

In this simple example, we're using the pandas library to read an Excel file into a DataFrame, which serves as the primary data structure in pandas. After that, we can implement sophisticated data analysis routines using Python's various scientific and data analysis libraries. Finally, the DataFrame's `to_excel` method lets us save the results back to Excel with the press of a button.

7.2c) "In Defense of Professional Reports: The Unseen Hero Behind Data Narratives"

In our exploration of Python and Excel powers, we unearth the real treasure - the capacity to generate professional reports. These reports, the unsung heroes in the saga of data analytics, turn tables of data into cohesive structures of knowledge. They form the backbone of professional data analysis, building a bridge between raw numbers and worthwhile insights.

Professional reports, furnished by Python's prowess and housed in Excel's familiar ambiance, streamline the chaos of numbers into an orchestra of information. They add a layer of sophistication and professionalism to your analysis – bolstering your narrative with hard facts, thoughtful analysis, and data-driven recommendations.

While Python amps up the report generation process, Excel serves as an efficient and easily accessible platform to design and disseminate these reports. The resulting combination is a highly effective, customizable, and user-friendly solution for diverse reporting needs. The days of manually updating Excel cells are behind us; Python script handles it all with automation and precision.

Geospatial Visualizations

The world of data becomes even more fascinating when we give it the power of location. Locational information or geospatial data, when visualised, uncovers patterns and narratives that are often hidden within raw data. Let us embark on the extraordinarily engaging journey of python-enchanted Excel and explore some fascinating geospatial visualizations.

Geospatial visualizations play a pivotal role in today's data-driven world. They not only provide context and appeal to massive datasets but also help detect spatial patterns and anomalies that can be challenging to identify in raw tabular data.

Python, with its extensive libraries like GeoPandas and Matplotlib, can handle a vast range of geospatial data operations with ease, from reading and writing geospatial data formats to performing geospatial operations and visualizations. Integrating these functionalities with Excel opens a whole new dimension of possibilities.

For instance, you can merge your geospatial data stored in Excel with geographies in a Shapefile using a common identifier, perform some analytics, and create gorgeous maps that are enticing as well as insightful.

Here's a simplified example:

```python
import geopandas as gpd
import pandas as pd

# Load your geospatial data from Shapefile
gdf = gpd.read_file("your_shape_file.shp")

# Load your data from Excel to DataFrame
df = pd.read_excel("your_data_file.xlsx")

# Merge geospatial and Excel data on a common identifier (ID)
merged = gdf.set_index('ID').join(df.set_index('ID'))

# Plot a choropleth map showing data distribution
merged.plot(column='your_variable',          cmap='YlOrRd',
legend=True)
```

In the example above, the GeoPandas library is used to read a Shapefile into a GeoDataFrame, and Panda's `read_excel` function is used to load Excel data into a DataFrame. The `set_index` and `join` functions are subsequently used to merge these two data sources based on a common identifier. Finally, the `plot` function from Matplotlib is used to generate an eye-catching choropleth map.

The globe maps we once reserved for geography classes and travel planning now boldly enter our spreadsheets, adding further zest to our data narratives. It's fascinating how geospatial visualizations bring our data down to earth, quite literally! They help us relate data stories to specific locations, lending a profound sense of reality and relevance.

Geospatial visualizations are not merely a fusion of data with maps. They are a confluence of curiosity and understanding, exploration and insight. As locations and attributes combine and interact, they birth compelling visual narratives that speak volumes, opening fresh perspectives and untapped opportunities.

By integrating Python's geospatial capabilities with Excel, we bring the world to our desks or even the palms of our hands. Excel, renowned for its simplicity, suddenly becomes a vehicle for immersive spatial exploration.

From geographical heatmaps and choropleths to route maps and 3D terrain profiles, Python enriched Excel breaks boundaries and expands horizons. The power to answer spatial questions, to visualize location-oriented hypotheses, and to explore geospatial patterns is truly intriguing.

Heatmaps and Conditional Formatting

When data dances into the realm of colours, it sings fascinating tales of trends, outliers, and gradients. This symphony of data and colours is usually orchestrated on a canvas we call a heatmap. Added to this, the baton of conditional formatting allows Excel to exhibit data in a sequence of shades representing numerical or categorical variance. Prepare to witness the rich ballet of heatmaps and conditional formatting, orchestrated through the combined powers of Python and Excel.

Heatmaps and conditional formatting are powerful tools that bring a third dimension to our two-dimensional table data.

They act as visual aids, highlighting patterns, variances, and correlations that are sometimes difficult to spot in large data sets.

Python, with its extensive support for data manipulation and visualizations through libraries such as Seaborn and Matplotlib, makes creating heatmaps straightforward. Seaborn, in particular, has a built-in heatmap plot that not only provides aesthetically pleasing default styles but also offers customization to a great extent.

For instance, creating a correlation heatmap using Seaborn is fairly simple:

```python
import seaborn as sns
import matplotlib.pyplot as plt
import pandas as pd

# Load your data from Excel to DataFrame
df = pd.read_excel("your_data_file.xlsx")

# Correlation matrix
corr_matrix = df.corr()

# Create a heatmap using Seaborn
sns.heatmap(corr_matrix, annot=True, cmap='coolwarm')
plt.show()
```

But the magic happens when Python hands this prowess over

to Excel. Python's pandas library enables us to export the data to Excel, while openpyxl or xlsxwriter can assign Excel's own "Conditional Formatting" to our data, generating heatmaps within the spreadsheet. It's like equipping Excel with a powerful, customizable colour palette, with Python scripting the art behind the scenes.

```python
import pandas as pd
from openpyxl import Workbook
from openpyxl.styles import Color, PatternFill
from openpyxl.utils.dataframe import dataframe_to_rows

# Load your data from Excel to DataFrame
df = pd.read_excel("your_data_file.xlsx")

# Create workbook and worksheet
wb = Workbook()
ws = wb.active

# Write DataFrame to worksheet
for r in dataframe_to_rows(df, index=False, header=True):
    ws.append(r)

# Define color gradient (red to green)
colors = ["FFFFFF", "FF0000", "FFFF00", "00FF00"]

# Apply conditional formatting
for row in ws.iter_rows(min_row=2, max_col=ws.max_column, max_row=ws.max_row):
```

```
    for cell in row:
        gradient_index = int(cell.value * (len(colors) - 1))
        fill = PatternFill(start_color=colors[gradient_index],
                    end_color=colors[gradient_index],
fill_type="solid")
        cell.fill = fill

wb.save("Heatmap.xlsx")
` ` `
```

7.4c) "The Colour-Coded Chronicles: Tales of Heatmaps and Conditional Formatting"

The chronicles of our data are now drafted in gradients of colour, distinguishing elements with an intuitive appeal and aiding the human eye to grasp patterns and outliers quickly. Heatmaps and conditional formatting are like painting our data with purpose, where colour shades are controlled by the significance of data values.

Heatmaps and conditional formatting bridge data comprehension and aesthetic visualization. They blend accuracy and intuition, empowering our decision making with the added dimension of visual cues. With Python propelling this in Excel, we have interlaced complex data manipulation with user-friendly visual simplicity.

The kaleidoscopic wonders of heatmaps and conditional formatting lend themselves wonderfully to multiple domains; from finance to science, healthcare to supply chain management. For instance, a financial analyst could produce a geographical heatmap representing market performance, or a biomedical scientist might generate a heatmap of genetic expressions.

Dynamic Charts

Every piece of data is a dot in an unseen painting, a note in an unheard symphony, a letter in an unwritten novel. When these dots, notes, and letters, meticulously brought together, start to move, we witness the artistry of dynamic charts. Imagine a financial trend that bristles with the pulsating share market, or a moving pie-chart that betrays the pattern of your spending over the month. Guided by Python and Excel, we are about to set these dots in motion.

Dynamic charts in Excel, fueled by Python, are a means to bring your data alive. They are interactive, making them a powerful tool to present complex data analysis. A dynamic chart can let users change the view of data interactively, like time period, categories, measures, and others, adding a significant dose of accessibility and comprehension to your reports.

Python's repertoire of data analysis libraries provides robust options for creating dynamic charts. A prominent one among them is plotly, an open-source library that lets you create visually appealing and interactive plots. The plots are rendered using web-based graphics, which makes them ideal for embedding in Jupyter notebooks or web applications.

Creating an interactive line chart, for instance, is as easy as:

```python
import plotly.graph_objs as go
import pandas as pd
```

```
# Load your data from Excel to DataFrame
df = pd.read_excel("your_data_file.xlsx")

# Create a line chart using Plotly
fig = go.Figure()

for column in df.columns:
    fig.add_trace(go.Scatter(x=df.index,          y=df[column],
    mode='lines', name=column))

fig.show()
```
`  ` `

This interactivity can then be brought right into Excel. One way to accomplish this is to export your dynamic visualizations created in Python into an HTML file and embed the HTML file into your Excel workbook using Excel's Web Browser control. While Python designs and details the movement, Excel delivers the interactive theatre to your audience.

With dynamic charts, your data is perpetually on a journey. It's not static, but in motion, constantly changing and updating based on the inputs it receives. It's a powerful way to visualize and understand the fluidness of your data, enabling you to see trends and patterns that would otherwise be obscured in a static visualization.

The integration of Python and Excel promises an array of functionalities – from elementary line graphs that track sales over time, to the complex scatter plots predicting future trends. Python's programming prowess fuels the functions, and Excel, with its interactive environment, serves as the perfect platform, making dynamic charts a joint masterpiece.

On the grand stage of Excel, your dynamic charts can assume various forms. In a stock market analysis, your dynamic line chart could track the daily fluctuations of share prices. If you are a project manager concerned about timelines, a dynamic Gantt chart integrating a series of tasks, in differing durations and sequences, would serve you well. Or maybe, you are a healthcare professional interested in knowing how your patient's vital signs are varying with time; A dynamic real-time plot would be your best companion.

With dynamic charts, data is no longer calculated; it is celebrated. Each chart is a waltz of facts around the stage of Excel, powered by the puppeteer of Python. As our exploration of the Python-Excel universe continues, let's await more surprising and intriguing revelations in the chapters to come.

Pivot Tables and Python

Pivot tables are akin to the grand architects of data summarization, sketching structured summaries from our raw data. Given the multidimensional analysis capability and ease of use, pivot tables have emerged as a jewel in Excel's crown. With Python by our side, we can twist and turn these data architects, making them craft masterpieces that adapt to our analytic needs.

Pivot tables in Excel are an essential tool for anyone working with data. They help summarize, analyze, explore, and present your data in an accessible manner. Their powerful 'drag and drop' interface means you can create flexible summaries and visualizations without even writing a single formula. This makes pivot tables an essential skill for anyone aiming to have a career in data science or analytics. Pivot tables don't only simplify data analysis but can also reveal hidden trends and patterns.

On the other hand, Python, as a high-level programming language, brings to the table a more dynamic and extensive approach to managing data. It offers libraries like pandas which allow us to handle large datasets and perform complex computations with simplicity. One of the key functionalities that pandas provides is a method to create pivot tables.

Creating a pivot table with pandas is as simple as this:

```python
import pandas as pd

# Load your data from Excel file to DataFrame
df = pd.read_excel('your_data_file.xlsx')

# Create a pivot table
pivot_table = pd.pivot_table(df, values='D', index='A', columns=['C'], aggfunc=np.sum)
print(pivot_table)
```

In this Python code, we read data from an Excel file into a DataFrame and then use the pivot_table function to create a pivot table. The parameters determine the structure of the pivot table. 'values' are the values to be aggregated, 'index' defines the rows of the pivot table, and 'columns' forms the columns. 'aggfunc' is the function to be used for aggregation, which in this case is the sum function provided by NumPy.

We can further customize this pivot table by adding a 'fill_value' parameter to replace NaN values, a 'margins' parameter to add a row/column subtotal or grand total, and a 'dropna' parameter to exclude categories with missing values.

Hence, with Python and pandas, transforming your raw data into a summarized pivot table is simple and straightforward. However, while working with Excel, the use of pivot tables doesn't stop there! They also serve as a basis for creating dynamic charts, conditional formatting, and interactive Excel dashboards.

Python and Excel mutually enhance each other's capabilities in a unique manner. Python brings the flexible and powerful computing and analytical capabilities. It allows you to get the data just the way you want it. At the same time, Excel leverages its powerful features like pivot tables, dynamic charts, and formatting to visualize and present the data interactively.

For instance, you can generate a pivot table using Python and pandas, and then use Excel to visualize this data. This can be easily accomplished by exporting the pivot table DataFrame to an Excel file using pandas' DataFrame.to_excel() method.

```python
pivot_table.to_excel('pivot_table.xlsx',      sheet_name='Pivot Table')
```

This Python script saves the pivot table as an Excel file, maintaining the pivot table format. The result is an Excel file that can be examined, analyzed, and portrayed using all of Excel's native capabilities.

This integration of Python with Excel's pivot tables not only opens new avenues of data summarization and visualization but also makes the process significantly more efficient and straightforward.

Python and Excel serve as a compelling combination for any financial analyst, data scientist, or anyone who deals with data. Python's robust computational abilities coupled with Excel's functional and user-friendly interface can arm you with the comprehensive toolkit you need to excel in the world of data analytics. With a good grasp of these tools, you'd be steps ahead in your journey of extracting insights and making informed decisions from your data.

Pivot tables uncover insights hidden in the nooks and crannies of raw, unprocessed data. By aiding in summarizing, slicing, dicing, and presenting our data in an understandable and visually pleasing manner, they play a pivotal role (pun intended!), in the discovery of our data story. Python, in this journey, is a loyal associate, enhancing, and empowering the process of crafting pivot tables.

For instance, suppose you're tasked with analyzing a dataset of a company's sales. The dataset is enormous, capturing every single sale over the past year, each with the date of sale, product, region, and sale amount. Now, your cliffhanging question is – "What product had the highest total sale in each region?" This mystery could remain unsolved with conventional data analysis and would require extensive formulas if Excel is used in isolation.

But with the Python and Excel integration, hand-in-hand with pandas' pivot table function, the answer could be unraveled in a matter of seconds:

```python
pivot_table = pd.pivot_table(df, values='Sale Amount', index='Region', columns='Product', aggfunc=np.sum)
```

Now, your resultant pivot table has the regions as rows, the products as columns, and the sum of sale amounts as values. Within a few minutes, you now have a structured summary that can answer your question at a glance.

Real-time Dashboard Updates

In this epoch of lightning-fast data flow, the world revolves around real-time data. Bringing this expediency to our Excel dashboards, Python enters the scene, infusing life with real-time updates. Much like a symphony orchestra that creates harmony in the midst of arrayed complexity, Python and Excel can orchestrate a grand ensemble of real-time dashboard updates.

Imagine watching a football match, but the scoreboard only updates once every hour. Your enjoyment is diminished as the real-time thrill is missing. This is how traditional dashboards, presenting static data, can feel like. With increasing data speed, there is an escalating need for dashboards that can keep up, dynamically updating in real time.

Excel dashboards are traditionally designed to present static overviews. Yet, with the right Python touch, they can be turned into active charts. This transformation allows Excel to display data as it streams in, painting the most recent picture of the metrics it represents.

To appreciate how Python scripts can breathe life into Excel dashboards, let's take the example of a stock market dashboard. It's designed to display the prices of selected stocks in real-time. A Python script can receive real-time data from a stock market API, process it, and then streamline it into Excel. This process transforms your static Excel dashboard into a real-time platform that continuously displays live stock market data.

Let's have a look at how this amazing feat can be achieved with Python code.

```python
import yfinance as yf
import openpyxl as xl

# Define the Excel file and worksheet
wb = xl.load_workbook('stock_dashboard.xlsx')
ws = wb['Sheet1']

# Define the stocks to watch
stocks = ['AAPL', 'MSFT', 'GOOGL']

# Continuous loop to update data
while True:
    row = 2
```

```
    for stock in stocks:
        # Get latest stock price
        ticker = yf.Ticker(stock)
        price = ticker.info['regularMarketPrice']

        # Write to Excel
        cell = f'B{row}'
        ws[cell] = price

        row += 1

    # Save the workbook
    wb.save('stock_dashboard.xlsx')
` ` `
```

This script starts by importing the necessary libraries - yfinance for getting the stock prices and openpyxl for writing the data into an Excel file. An infinite loop ensures the updating is continuous while the code inside the loop fetches the real-time price of each stock through yfinance and writes it into the Excel worksheet 'Sheet1'.

The magic happens with the 'while True' loop. In Python, a 'while' loop continues executing its block of code as long as its condition remains true. Since 'True' is always true by definition, the loop will continue indefinitely, providing a consistent flow of real-time data to your Excel dashboard.

Crucially, the updates are not delayed or sporadic but happen in real-time, giving you the power to make timely decisions based on the most up-to-date data.

Real-time dashboard updates deliver the power to eliminate guesswork and make informed decisions in real-time. Python serves as the invisible conductor of this orchestra, pulsating with the rhythm of data and the beats of Excel. Discovering the melody in the chaos, the combination of Python and Excel shatters limitations, transforming static representations into dynamic masterpieces of real-time updates.

Another practical use case of Python empowering real-time updates in Excel dashboards is in social media analytics. As social media platforms generate vast amounts of data, businesses are keen to analyze this information in real-time and draw actionable insights.

For instance, a company may want to monitor the engagement metrics of their latest social media posts across different platforms on an Excel dashboard. Python can fetch this data in real-time via API calls to these platforms. As the audience engagement changes every second across the globe, the business can see these changes reflect in their Excel dashboard live.

Here is a simplified Python code example of how this could be facilitated, using Twitter's API as a hypothetical example:

```python
import tweepy
import openpyxl as xl

# Initialize API using your access details
auth      =      tweepy.OAuthHandler('your_consumer_key',
'your_consumer_secret')
```

```
auth.set_access_token('your_access_token',
'your_access_token_secret')

api = tweepy.API(auth)

# Define the Excel file and worksheet
wb = xl.load_workbook('tweet_dashboard.xlsx')
ws = wb['Sheet1']

# Define the tweet to monitor
tweet_id = '123456789'

# Continuous loop to update data
while True:
    # Use Twitter API to get tweet details
    tweet_status = api.get_status(tweet_id)
    retweet_count = tweet_status.retweet_count
    like_count = tweet_status.favorite_count

    # Update Excel
    ws['B2'] = retweet_count
    ws['B3'] = like_count

    # Save the workbook
    wb.save('tweet_dashboard.xlsx')
```

This script fetches the number of retweets and likes for a specific tweet in real-time and writes the data into an Excel file. Combining the efficiency of Python and familiarity of Excel, businesses can now have a real-time overview of their social media engagement.

The integration of Python and Excel opens the door to a world where data is no longer static, but dynamic, updating continuously and painting an evolving picture. As the maestro of real-time dashboard updates, Python's versatility infuses vigor into Excel dashboards, enabling them to pivot on the tip of the real-time data wave. Thus, when working in tandem, Python and Excel sing a symphony that echoes in the realms of real-time data analytics, enabling decision-makers to glean the most timely insights.

CHAPTER 8: OPTIMIZING PERFORMANCE AND EFFICIENCY IN EXCEL WITH PYTHON

Performance Optimization Techniques

In the quest for speed and efficiency, it is vital to optimize our Python-Excel workflows. Here, we will examine a bouquet of performance optimization techniques that can allow your Python and Excel integrations to become evermore nimble and agile, resembling a sprinter ready to break world records effortlessly.

Efficiency is the soul of high-performing code. When it comes to the integration of Python and Excel, optimization plays a crucial role in how quickly and effectively we can process vast amounts of data. There are multiple strategies we can employ to improve and trim our Python-Excel operations, making sure we are maximizing our resources to deliver top-tier performance in our tasks.

One of the key performance-hogging areas in Python-Excel operations is the process of writing data to Excel cells. Conventionally, you may be tempted to write individual data to cells one at a time, using a loop, especially when dealing with complex data structures. However, this isn't the most efficient method. The reason being, each write operation requests Excel's computational resources, leading to higher waiting times as each operation has to finish before the next begins.

```python
# Traditional non-optimized way
wb = openpyxl.Workbook()
ws = wb.active

for i, element in enumerate(data, start=1):
    ws.cell(row=i, column=1, value=element)

wb.save('data.xlsx')
```

In the above script, we are writing data to cells one after the other. When dealing with larger data, the execution speed can be slow due to waiting times between each operation.

A faster and more efficient way is to harness 'batch operations'. Instead of writing data to Excel one cell at a time, we can write in batches, significantly reducing the waiting times and enhancing the execution speed.

```python
# Optimized way using batch operations
```

```
wb = openpyxl.Workbook()
ws = wb.active

for row_id, element in enumerate(data, start=1):
    ws.cell(row=row_id, column=1).value = element

wb.save('data.xlsx')
```
` ` `

In this optimized version, the entire data list is written to the Excel sheet in one go, massively improving the speed.

Apart from optimizing write operations, one can make use of Python's built-in functionality to speed up calculations. For instance, if you are processing large datasets with Python before pushing the results into Excel, consider using vectorization techniques with libraries like NumPy instead of performing calculations in for-loops.

Next, you want to make sure you're saving your Excel files only when necessary. Each save operation can be expensive in terms of time and resources. If you're carrying out a series of operations, consider saving once after all operations are complete, rather than after each operation.

Lastly, consider the usage of data structures. Python dictionaries are known for their fast lookup times, and using them for storing and accessing data can often be more efficient than using lists or other data types.

Relishing the thrill of speed, Performance Optimization techniques fine-tune our Python and Excel operations, turning them into racing steeds that gallop robustly amidst the world of data. Harnessing these techniques, we command the wheels of efficiency, steering our data drive to its peak operational potential for exceptional Python-Excel integrations.

Python's ability to interact with Excel through libraries like openpyxl or Pandas is a major advantage to data analysts who want to leverage both Python's power and Excel's ease. However, moving large amounts of data between Python and Excel could become slow if not optimized properly. Hence, being mindful of the data we need to parse and the operations we perform can save valuable time.

```python
# Optimized way using Pandas
import pandas as pd

# Load the Excel file
df = pd.read_excel('data.xlsx')

# Perform operations
df['column2'] = df['column1'] * 2

# Save back to Excel
df.to_excel('data.xlsx', index=False)
```

In this optimized process using Pandas, we are loading the entire Excel file as a DataFrame, performing side operations, and then saving it back once. This method utilizes batch operations at both ends - loading and saving - and improves performance in comparison to writing and reading cell by cell.

With the raw power of Python and the user-friendly interface of Excel, their integration offers an empowering platform for data operation. By incorporating performance optimization techniques, we move beyond mere possibility towards achieving unprecedented efficiency. It is akin to transforming an exquisite piece of music into an impressive symphony, fulfilling the pursuit of excellence and scalability in Python-Excel data operations.

Handling Large Datasets

Handling large datasets is akin to taming wild beasts - a task demanding both finesse and skill. When Python-Excel integration is our arena, we need to know the best strategies and tools to manage these data-loaded giants with expertise. Here, we shall journey through the nuances of handling large datasets efficiently in the Python-Excel interface.

Managing large datasets is a common challenge for data professionals globally. When working within the Python-Excel interface, one can meet this challenge with a robust toolbox of techniques designed to tame dense datasets effectively. These approaches aim at optimizing memory usage, reducing computational need, and maintaining performance levels despite the increasing data volume.

One basic approach to handle large datasets is through chunking. Rather than loading an entire dataset into memory, we can load and process it in smaller, manageable pieces or chunks. Python's Pandas library offers a flexible and efficient way for this.

```python
```

```
# Load data in chunks

chunksize = 1000

for     chunk     in        pd.read_excel("large_dataset.xlsx",
chunksize=chunksize):

    process(chunk)
```

In this example, pandas read_excel method reads the data in chunks. The chunk size can be adjusted according to the system's memory and the size of the dataset.

Another powerful tool for handling large datasets is using Pandas's 'category' data type. It is especially useful when we have repetitive text values in a column. Converting such a column to type 'category' can significantly reduce the memory usage.

```python
# Using category data type

df["column"] = df["column"].astype("category")
```

Python also shines in handling large datasets through its multiprocessing capabilities. By dividing the dataset processing tasks among multiple processors, Python can perform several tasks simultaneously, harnessing the full power of the system's processor cores. This stands to sharply decrease the processing times handling large datasets.

However, when dealing with Excel, we face a limitation. Excel cannot perform multiprocessing operations inherently. To circumvent this, we can again use Python's prowess. The Python Excel libraries, such as openpyxl or xlrd, allow us to read Excel files outside the Excel environment, benefit from

Python's multiprocessing capabilities, and then write back the processed data to Excel.

Also, Python's libraries come with functions optimized for large datasets. Functions from libraries such as NumPy, SciPy, or Pandas often outperform their counterparts from Excel in terms of performance and scalability when dealing with large datasets.

While Python provides the firepower to handle large datasets, Excel offers the perfect interface to summarize and visualize the results of our analysis by creating charts, pivot tables, and conditional formats without requiring extensive programming.

Essentially, handling large datasets does not have to be a dreadful chore if we know how to optimize Python functions, manage memory, and leverage Python's multiprocessing capabilities effectively when operating within the Python-Excel ecosystem.

As we unveil the power of Python and Excel, large datasets are no longer daunting but become intriguing puzzles to solve. Crafting our skills in data handling, we realize that no dataset is too large to tackle. Embracing the concepts discussed, we can navigate through the vast seas of data with confidence, thus capturing the true essence of this fantastical Python-Excel harmonization.

Looking after large datasets, whether in Python or Excel, is akin to being a good shepherd. You need the right tools for the job, and you need to know how to use them properly. Python is your staff, guiding you through the data wilderness, while

Excel is your loyal sheepdog, rounding up stray variables and ensuring that all your data is present and correct.

While Python is excellent at managing large amounts of data, Excel doesn't always work as comfortably with a high volume of variables. Here, offloading the processing work to Python can prove beneficial. Python's diverse libraries, like Pandas or NumPy, offer multi-threading and synchronous execution capabilities, which are handy when dealing with a plethora of data.

By processing large datasets in Python and transferring the output to Excel, you can benefit from Python's functionality and Excel's accessibility. Always remember, proper data handling, no matter how large, lies at the heart of any well-functioning Python-Excel integration.

Memory Management

Much like a foggy morning that you must navigate through, memory management can often loom as an overwhelming concept in the Python-Excel integration framework. However, with suitable strategies and a keen understanding of how Python and Excel handle memory, we can chart this terrain effectively. In this engaging exploration, we lattice through memory management's crucial aspects within Python-Excel ecosystem.

In managing memory within a Python-Excel integration environment, understanding the distinct ways that Python and Excel handle memory usage becomes paramount. Python, being a memory-managed language, takes care of most memory-related tasks under the hood. However, explicitly stating a variable or object to None allows Python's built-in garbage collector to free up the memory sooner. The memory that Python interprets uses is allocated from a private heap, and Python takes care of making sure things aren't left out too long.

In comparison, Excel loads an entire workbook into memory when opened. If you're dealing with large data sets, this might result in plentiful inefficiencies. However, Excel offers methods, such as ActiveX Data Objects (ADO), which allow to connect to Excel workbooks as a data source and allows partial loading of data.

Applying these understanding to memory optimized Python codes and Excel usage can significantly improve the efficiency of Python-Excel projects.

Within Python, one useful approach in memory management is to use data storage structures that are more efficient in memory usage. For example, instead of using lists, numpy arrays or pandas dataframes can be used. They are significantly more memory efficient as these structures store data in contiguous blocks of memory.

```python
# Using NumPy for memory efficiency
import numpy as np
data = np.array([1, 2, 3, 4, 5])
```

In this example, the NumPy array is much more memory-efficient compared to a corresponding Python list.

Pandas offer a similar advantage when dealing with large and complex datasets. They provide memory-efficient data structures along with intuitive data manipulation functions.

Python generators can also be effectively used to manage memory. Generators are special functions that return a lazy iterator, which means they generate values on the fly rather than storing them in memory.

```python
# Python generator example
def large_dataset_generator(n):
    num = 0
    while num < n:
        yield num
        num += 1
```

In this case, the generator function generates one number at a time instead of creating an entire list in memory.

A powerful method in memory management in Python is the garbage collector. Python's garbage collector is proficient at managing memory, but sometimes manually invoking it can be beneficial. The gc module can be used to interface with the garbage collector.

```python
# Interacting with the garbage collector
import gc

gc.collect()
```

This command cleans up objects that are no longer in use. However, this command should be used sparingly as it may decrease performance.

For Excel add-ins developed using Python, avoiding loading entire datasets into Excel memory can be achieved using Python's xlwings library. Connecting Excel to Python as an external data source allows Excel to load data only when necessary, significantly reducing memory usage.

Conclusively, memory management for Python-Excel interfacing requires understanding of both Python and Excel's memory handling nature. Using memory-friendly Python constructs and intelligently loading data into Excel can optimize memory usage, resulting in projects that scale and perform well.

We can now see memory management in the Python-Excel realm as a manageable affair rather than a daunting maze. Like decoding a matrix, understanding how Python and Excel handle memory and use it efficiently can significantly improve our program's performance. With the right approach, this newfound clarity can be instrumental in navigating through the foggy alleyways of memory terrain in Python-Excel integration, a challenging yet rewarding endeavor.

Parallel Processing

At the intersection of Python and Excel integration, we uncover the thoroughfare of parallel processing - a pathway notorious for bolstering computational speed like none other. This lane is not for the faint-hearted. Herein, multiple tasks simultaneously gallop across the multiple available cores, manoeuvring a marked leap towards efficiency. Together in our journey, we are about to unravel the methodologies of harnessing the power of parallel processing in Python-Excel integration.

The charm of parallel processing is its fundamental doctrine - 'Why go alone, when we can harness the power of togetherness?' By dividing a large task into several sub-tasks that can run concurrently, parallel processing provides a substantial speed boost when dealing with large datasets or complex calculations.

In the realm of Python, there exists a multitude of libraries that support parallel processing, the most common being multiprocessing, threading, and concurrent.futures.

The multiprocessing module capitalises on the multiple cores in the CPU and bypasses the Global Interpreter Lock (GIL), a mechanism that prevents multiple native threads from executing Python bytecodes simultaneously. As a result, it can execute processes on different cores simultaneously, perfect for CPU-bound tasks.

```python
from multiprocessing import Pool
def square(number):
    return number * number

if __name__ == '__main__':
    numbers = [1,2,3,4,5]
    p = Pool()
    result = p.map(square, numbers)
    p.close()
```

```
    p.join()
```

In this sample code, we create a worker pool and map our square function to the input data, parallelizing the square operation across the different cores of our CPU.

Threading is beneficial when you have a lot of I/O-bound tasks, that is when your task is waiting creatively for input or output operations, and you could be doing something else while waiting.

```python
import threading

def print_square(number):
    print('Square:', number * number)

def print_cube(number):
    print('Cube:', number * number * number)

if __name__ == '__main__':
    t1 = threading.Thread(target=print_square, args=(10,))
    t2 = threading.Thread(target=print_cube, args=(10,))

    t1.start()
    t2.start()

    t1.join()
    t2.join()
```

In this snippet, we start two threads concurrently, each performing a different operation. The `join()` method ensures that the main program waits for both threads to finish before proceeding.

The concurrent.futures library provides a higher-level interface for using multiprocessing and threading. It provides a common interface for both threading and multiprocessing using an Executor object.

```python
from concurrent.futures import ThreadPoolExecutor

def square(number):
    return number * number

if __name__ == '__main__':
    numbers = [1,2,3,4,5]
    with ThreadPoolExecutor() as executor:
        results = executor.map(square, numbers)
```

Here, we use a ThreadPoolExecutor to parallelize our square function across various threads.

In terms of Excel integration, parallel processing can be particularly useful when handling large datasets and running complex, time-consuming operations. For instance, we could parallelize operations such as data fetching, cleaning, analyses, or generation of complex simulations, allowing Excel to squeeze the maximum performance out of today's multi-core processors while working with large datasets.

Remember, parallel processing isn't always the right solution. It comes with its own overhead — the time taken to spawn and manage multiple processes or threads. Therefore, the suitability of parallel processing is highly dependent on the task at hand.

The mastery of parallel processing in Python-Excel integration grants us command over several lanes. By catapulting processes and tasks across multiple cores concurrently, we alter the landscape of computational efficiency, turning apparent bottlenecks into superhighways of execution. Thus, weaving the power of Python with Excel's potency, we inadvertently spearhead the art of multitasking, channelling raw data through our calculations at a speed resonating with light. Regardless of the complexity, mastering this art propels us further into the realm of excellence, encasing our prowess in both Python and Excel. This combination, once achieved, allows us to become true shapers of data, masters of information, in an ever-advancing digital age.

Caching Techniques

As we journey through the dynamic world of Python and Excel integration, we stumble upon an intriguing technique that promises an efficient boost - caching. An intelligent bridging mechanism in the computational realm, caching ensures the swift execution of repeated operations. It enables us to store and retrieve already computed results, saving valuable computational time. Eager to explore further? Let's plunge into caching's nuts and bolts and how it bolsters our Python-Excel integration arsenal.

The principal idea behind caching is exceptionally simple: why calculate the same thing several times when you can calculate it once, store the result, and use it again whenever needed? This is where Python steps in with an elegant, built-in solution - the lru_cache decorator from the functools module. Python's lru_cache (Least Recently Used Cache) is a decorator that allows us to wrap our functions and store their return values for a given set of parameters.

```python
# Import required library
from functools import lru_cache

# Apply caching to our function
@lru_cache(maxsize=None)
def expensive_operation(n):
    # Assume this operation takes a long time to execute
    return n * n
```

In this instance, the `maxsize` argument defines the maximum size of our cache. If `maxsize` is set to `None`, the LRU feature is disabled, and our cache can grow without bounds.

Now, when we call `expensive_operation` with the same arguments, Python will not compute the operation but fetch the result from the cache. We've saved time and resources!

One thing to note, however, is that lru_cache only works if the function we're wrapping is 'pure' - that is, it does not have side effects, and its output only depends on its input.

Unfortunately, Excel doesn't have built-in support for caching, but through Python and VBA, we can implement some forms of it. For example, in VBA, we could use a dictionary to store calculated values as we go, mimicking some cache behavior.

In the context of Python-Excel integration, you'll find caching to be incredibly useful in scenarios involving repeated complex calculations. For instance, consider a financial forecasting model in Excel, which uses a third-party API to fetch market data. Each API request could take substantial time, and if we are running multiple iterations, the total wait time could be considerable. However, caching the results of each request means subsequent iterations that need the same data can fetch it almost instantly.

```python
# Import required library
from functools import lru_cache

# Apply caching to our function
@lru_cache(maxsize=None)
def get_market_data(security):
    # Assume this operation is slow, such as making an API request
    pass
```

In this example, if we call `get_market_data(security)` for the same security multiple times across various Excel cells, Python will not make the API call every time. Instead, on subsequent calls, Python will retrieve the price from the cache.

One must tread cautiously, though, as caching is not always the correct solution. With large datasets or heavy computations, caching every single result can quickly consume your available memory. To avoid this, you can limit cache size using the `maxsize` parameter of the lru_cache decorator or ensure you clear your cache when the calculated values are no longer needed.

Caching, in the Python-Excel integration landscape, unveils a resilient fast-track, a computational catalyst that flaunts unmatched efficiency. This clever technique harbours the potential to transform function calls, irrespective of their trajectories, into instantaneous retrievals. It snips away redundant pursuits, reinstating computation power to where it arguably belongs - solving new mysteries of our data. By employing caching, our Python-Excel integration quite literally learns from the past, exploiting prior accomplishments to spur future expeditions, thereby ensuring that no calculation, once mastered, has to be grappled with again. Thus, with caching, we escalate our momentum, soaring from a trodden walk towards a spirited sprint in our Python-Excel journey.

Error Handling

The pristine perfection of a well-oiled machine is indeed the mark of an expertly crafted system, but true finesse lies in preparing for the unexpected. When Python and Excel mesh gears in your analytical engine, any unexpected jolts or stalls demand a fine-tuned mechanism to manage those contingencies proficiently. We pivot our attention next to error handling - an essential, albeit often sidelined, aspect of a robust Python-Excel integrated system. Let's delve deep into this essential facet and comprehend how Python and Excel handle errors and the techniques to form a reliable error handling mechanism.

While most coding endeavors are focused on creating and implementing logical solutions to problems at hand, the reality of programming also comprises a significant share of 'disaster management'. Errors and exceptions are an integral part of the coding universe. But don't fret – Python, with its comprehensive built-in exceptions and error handling mechanisms, equips you to handle them gracefully.

```python
try:
    # risky operation
    result = x / y
except ZeroDivisionError:
    print('Division by zero is not allowed.')
else:
    print('Operation was successful.')
finally:
    print('Cleaning up resources.')
```

In the code snippet above, Python's `try`-`except` block covers risky operations. If an error occurs, the `except` clause is executed. The error type, `ZeroDivisionError` in this case, can be named as well. The `else` clause runs if no exception appears, while the `finally` clause always executes, providing an ideal place for clean-up tasks.

Python encourages using `try`-`except` blocks early and

often for better program flow and error handling. A rule of thumb is to extract problematic code sections to functions and wrap those calls inside `try`-`except` blocks. Functions with specific tasks provide a higher likelihood of handling any exceptions they might raise.

Excel can also handle errors with the `IFERROR` function. Excel lacks Python's advanced error handling but in data manipulation, `IFERROR` can manage widespread issues. However, this is limited to certain Excel actions.

```excel
=IFERROR(A1/B1, "Error Message")
```

On another front, VBA allows advanced error handling similar to Python but is esoteric and used less frequently. Yet, knowledge of VBA error handling may bestow advantages in niche cases.

Despite their powerful individual mechanisms, the integration of Python and Excel may still confront unforeseen errors. For instance, suppose Python is reading an Excel file while another user is editing it. A common error is 'Permission Denied,' which only arises during reading or writing to the file. Python's `PermissionError` exception can handle this gracefully.

Python-Excel integration supports us further by interacting directly with Excel through libraries like `xlwings` and `openpyxl`. It allows us to probe Excel data, run Pythonic error checks, and fix issues. This approach can avoid errors that might jam Excel alone, rendering clean error-free data.

Consider that you are using Python to read Excel files filled out by users. Excel may mark cells with non-date data as a date format, tricking Python during reading. A Python function to verify date data is advisable to avoid errors downstream.

```python
from dateutil.parser import parse

def is_date(string):
    try:
        parse(string)
        return True
    except ValueError:
        return False
```

In this example, `dateutil.parser.parse` tries to parse the string into a date. If it fails, a `ValueError` is raised, and the function returns `False`.

As we integrate Python and Excel, the error handling strategy should be bifocal - handling Python and Excel errors. It ensures our Python-Excel integration modules are robust and reliable, leading to smoother workflows and insightful data analysis results.

The path to mastery in any sphere inevitably entails encountering and overcoming hurdles. Error handling, therefore, is not merely an auxiliary tool but a fundamental cornerstone reinforcing our Python-Excel integration framework's robustness. Its ability to preempt the unpredictable and mitigate potential setbacks morphs our analytical journey from a bumpy ride into a seamlessly smooth voyage. Hence, error handling, with its salvage mechanisms, liberates us from perpetual worry over prospective errors. It permits us to channel our cerebral might toward our end objective, secure in knowing that we are well-equipped to face any adversarial contingencies that come our way.

Thus, as we blend Python's power and Excel's elegance, we construct not only an algorithmic marvel but also a resilient analytical fortress, safeguarded against unexpected anomalies.

API Rate Limiting and Optimization

At the confluence of Python and Excel, the mesmerizing dance of data enriches our analytical bouquet. Yet, obstacles are bound to pepper the path of any worthwhile endeavor. One such challenge we encounter, especially when Python interacts with APIs to pull data into Excel, is dealing with API rate limits. Just as a riveting mystery novel doesn't disclose everything at once, APIs too, have their thresholds. Lets turn our lens to understand the nuances of API rate limiting and strategies to optimize interactions with APIs along this Python-Excel bridge.

Data streaming has become a ubiquitous phenomenon thanks to APIs, the ever-vigilant sentinels that mediate the free flow of information across the internet. But, APIs are more than mere communication channels. They are the gatekeepers that control access to valuable data. APIs employ a throttle mechanism, commonly known as 'rate limiting,' which restricts the frequency of requests by a client in a specific time frame.

In simpler terms, the API tells every client - 'There's plenty of data for everyone, but let's not get overzealous. Take it easy.'

Rate limits ensure all API users have equal access and prevent spamming. Each API could have different rules. Some allow a certain number of requests per day, a few others limit requests every hour or minute. Hence, it's crucial to understand the limit specifications of the API you are using before incorporating it into your Python code.

Nevertheless, Python, with its versatile and resourceful repository of modules, bestows us with the ability to handle rate limiting gracefully. Python's `ratelimiter` module is a brilliant tool in tackling this use case.

Below is a simple example showcasing the use of Python's rate limiter for a hypothetical API call.

```python
from ratelimiter import RateLimiter
import requests

@RateLimiter(max_calls=10, period=1)
def api_call():
    response = requests.get('https://api.example.com/data')
    return response.json()
```

In this example, using the `RateLimiter` decorator before the `api_call` function ensures that the function doesn't exceed more than ten calls per second. This decorator is a prudent and efficient way to respect rate limiting concerns and avoid misusing API resources simultaneously.

Another practical tool is Python's `time` module, where developers often use the `time.sleep` function in their code to pause execution for a specified number of seconds. This pause can slow the request rate and help stay within API rate limits.

```python
import time
import requests

for i in range(100):
    response = requests.get('https://api.example.com/data')
    time.sleep(0.1) # pause for 100 milliseconds
```

This practice can be helpful, but it should be used judiciously. Overuse can lead to unnecessarily slow programs and inefficient API utilization. It's essential to balance the fine line between respecting API rate limits and availing the maximum data within those parameters.

When it comes to optimizing your Python code, there are several things to keep in mind. When an API interaction involves large chunks of data, considering how requests are structured can make a significant difference.

- **Batching**: It's often more efficient to send fewer requests that pull in a lot of data, rather than many requests for small amounts of data. For APIs that allow it, request as much data as possible per call to reduce the number of calls.

- **Pagination**: For APIs that return data in pages, ensure that each page contains as much data as the API allows. This minimizes requests and reduces pagination overhead.

- **Concurrency**: If an API allows, make multiple requests concurrently to reduce waiting time. Python's threading or asyncio libraries are excellent tools for such purposes.

- **Caching**: Store API responses to reduce unnecessary requests. This works best for data that doesn't change frequently.

Negotiating API restrictions is much about staying respectful of shared resources and API providers' rules. Thankfully, with Python's sophisticated error-handling mechanism and Excel's compatibility, the integration boasts effective API rate limiting and optimization techniques.

When Python scripts interact with APIs to weave complex arrays of data into Excel sheets, the high-tech symphony doesn't play without its notes of discord. API rate limiting, a common restriction, disrupts the harmonious duet, yet plays a vital role in maintaining a spacious landscape for all data enthusiasts. But worry not, for difficulty is merely the predecessor of brilliance. Like tuning a diverse orchestra for an immersive melody, Python and Excel equip us with the tools to harmonize with API rate limits, ensuring that our analytical concerto remains compelling. By adopting practiced strategies and respecting shared spaces of the internet, we can safely navigate around these hurdles and continue our waltz with data, driven by the vibrant tunes of insights and wisdom.

CHAPTER 9: WEB SCRAPING AND API INTEGRATION WITH PYTHON AND EXCEL

Introduction to Web Scraping

In the vast and dynamic landscape of data, the pageantry of numbers and characters, lies a wealth of transformative insights. Python, Excel, and you, the eager explorer, begin to embark on a thrilling trek into the life-infused jungle of web scraping. When Python and Excel come together, they morph into an extraordinary data-expedition charter, navigating the labyrinth of information and orchestrating a symphony of valuable insights from the random notes scattered across the internet. In this exciting chapter, we will put on our explorer hats, tread the ingenious trail of web scraping, and demystify the nuts and bolts of this powerful data extraction technique.

Web scraping is akin to mining for digital gold. It allows us to excavate valuable information from the extensive reserves of the worldwide web. But what exactly is web scraping? In simple terms, web scraping is a method to extract information from websites systematically. It is the process of automating the human exploration of the World Wide Web, either using algorithms that simulate human exploration or directly using the HTTP protocol.

As a tool, Python, with its rich variety of libraries such as BeautifulSoup, Scrapy, and Selenium, provides a robust foundation for web scraping. And when coupled with Excel, a powerful data analysis and visualization tool, it offers a dynamic blend of vast data acquisition and meaningful data interpretation.

Let's look at a simple example of web scraping with Python using the BeautifulSoup library. The below code retrieves the HTML of a webpage and prints the title tag content.

```python
from bs4 import BeautifulSoup
import requests

url = 'https://www.example.com'
response = requests.get(url)
soup = BeautifulSoup(response.text, 'html.parser')
print(soup.title.string)
```

In the realm of business, finance, or any data-driven field, web scraping can be a boon. From generating leads to conducting market research, web scraping provides a creative solution to a myriad of challenges. It opens a gateway to capture real-time data for making timely decisions. This comes in handy, especially in volatile sectors like financial markets. By collating data directly from various sources, financial models feeding into Excel sheets become more accurate and prolific.

However, while the benefits are substantial, web scraping is not without its caveats. Numerous ethical and legal considerations need to be taken into account.

Firstly, ensure that the data being scraped is public and the website owner approves of it. Many sites have 'robots.txt' files to clarify what data is open for scraping. It's always advisable to consult this file before proceeding with the data extraction.

Secondly, look at the frequency of your scraping. Bombarding a website with too frequent requests can lead to being blocked. By adding time delays and respecting the site's rate limits, you demonstrate ethical behavior while securing your ability to scrape the site in the future.

Here's an example code snippet demonstrating how to be respectful by limiting the frequency of hits:

```python
from bs4 import BeautifulSoup
import requests
import time

url = 'https://www.example.com'
time.sleep(1) - # wait for a second before making a request
response = requests.get(url)
soup = BeautifulSoup(response.text, 'html.parser')
print(soup.title.string)
```

Finally, the extracted data use and distribution should comply with all relevant privacy policies. Misuse of data, particularly personal information, is a breach of privacy and can necessitate legal complications.

The sphere of web scraping is a vast, enriching field, pulsating with potential. Its power to arm Excel with a vast array of real-time data is nothing short of revolutionary. However, the task is complex and delicate, needing a fine balance between technical proficiency and ethical awareness. As with any powerful tool, the key is in understanding its purpose, exploring its potential, and exercising discretion and responsibility in its usage.

Into the limitless expanse of the digital universe, Python and Excel embark on an exciting adventure – web scraping. This dynamic duo presents not just a method to extract information from the internet but an innovative approach to discovering, learning, and transforming the raw, unorganised, and often perplexing world of web data into a meaningful analytical masterpiece. As the Python-Excel maestro, you have the baton to conduct this fascinating symphony of data extraction and transformation, illuminating the concealed insights amid the sprawling web chaos. So lets brave this voyage into the fascinating realm of web scraping, where each web page turned unravels a new chapter of wisdom and understanding.

Working with RESTful APIs:

From the cosmic orchestra of the internet, comes the melodious rhythm of RESTful APIs, weaving the mystical notes of data into a harmonious concert. As Python and Excel enthusiasts, we enter the fascinating world of APIs, highly intrigued and eager to decrypt this potent source of information. Here, we will delve deep into the mesmerizing enigma of RESTful APIs, scripting the symphony of Python and Excel to perform this resounding piece of real-time data interaction with the grandeur it deserves.

In the concert of internet data flow, APIs find their place as the composers, orchestrating a beautifully synchronized stream of communication. APIs, or Application Programming Interfaces, are the conduits that enable different software applications to interact with each other. Among the various types of APIs, RESTful or Representational State Transfer APIs have found favor due to their simplicity, scalability, and stateless operations.

RESTful APIs adhere to the standard HTTP methods using URLs, and they typically return data in JSON (JavaScript Object Notation) format. This makes them particularly attractive for Python-based web scraping, as Python has excellent support for JSON data through its json library.

But how does this work hand-in-hand with Excel? Quite simply, Excel becomes the stage where the symphony is performed. It is in Excel's grid that the data, procured and processed through Python and APIs, finally takes shape and meaning.

To start working with RESTful APIs in Python, there are several libraries that you can use - requests, httplib2, treq, and more. The requests library, with its intuitive and easy-to-use functions, is particularly popular.

Consider the below Python snippet using the requests library to GET data from a RESTful API:

```python
import requests
import json

response = requests.get('https://api.example.com/data')
data = response.json()

# Now, let's say you want to store this data in an Excel sheet

import pandas as pd

df = pd.DataFrame(data)
df.to_excel('data.xlsx', index = False)
```

The above code performs a GET request using the API's URL and converts the response, typically a JSON object, into a Python dictionary using the .json() method. Then, it uses the Pandas library to convert this dictionary into a data frame - a two-dimensional tabular data structure that can then be easily written into an Excel file.

In light of the finance domain, understanding and employing RESTful APIs prove particularly advantageous. They allow direct access to real-time stock prices, financial reports, and economic indicators. This data, coupled with Excel's data analysis capabilities, aids in making strategic financial decisions, running potent models, and generating detailed reports.

In practice, several financial market platforms like Alpha

Vantage, IEX Cloud, and Polygon offer APIs that return various market data. Here's an example of how you could use Alpha Vantage's API to retrieve real-time foreign exchange (FX) rates and store them in an Excel file:

```python
import requests
import json
import pandas as pd

# Replace 'your_api_key' with your actual API key
response = requests.get('https://www.alphavantage.co/query?function=CURRENCY_EXCHANGE_RATE&from_currency=USD&to_currency=JPY&apikey=your_api_key')
data = response.json()['Realtime Currency Exchange Rate']

df = pd.DataFrame(data, index=[0])
df.to_excel('FX_rates.xlsx', index = False)
```

Yet, it's vital to remember that the use of APIs, much like web scraping, carries with it a responsibility. It is required to respect API usage policies, including rate limits and data usage terms. Too many requests in a short span may lead to being blocked or, in some cases, accrued charges.

Mastering RESTful APIs is a reward in itself. It's a journey through the real-time world of data, a journey made even more significant by the power of Python and Excel. As finance professionals, the ability to harness this power will undoubtedly equip us with valuable tools for data-driven decision-making.

RESTful APIs, a beautiful segment of our data symphony, play an integral role in facilitating the seamless harmony between our invaluable Python and Excel capabilities. They serve as the note sheets, directing the flow and pace of our data concert. As we draw the curtains on our insightful exploration of RESTful APIs, we can't help but appreciate the enormous potential they unlock in the realm of real-time data access. From illuminating intricate financial insights to shaping investment strategies, the application of RESTful APIs marks a significant step forward in our Python-Excel journey. So let's continue to embrace this learning expedition, painting our masterpiece on the canvas that the Python-Excel palette presents to us.

OAuth and Token-based Authentication

Just as a captivating symphony would be incomplete without a captivating encore, our journey through Python and Excel's integration with APIs would be incomplete without delving into the intricacies of OAuth and token-based authentication.

In authentication's dramatic play, OAuth and token-based systems play the heroic protagonists, safeguarding our data rendezvous with a cloak of encryption. OAuth, or Open Authorization, is an open standard for secure access delegation that facilitates users' approval of applications accessing their information without exposing their credentials. Expressly, with APIs requiring an access token to accept any communication from Python, encryption enters our Python-Excel play, adding a thrilling twist.

OAuth is an interoperable protocol that allows secure

authorization in a simple, standardized way for web, mobile, and desktop applications. OAuth protocol mediates between the application (client), the user, and the service, providing the client with an access token for the server in response to the resource owner's authorization. Crucially, the protocol is manipulated in the retrieval of this token, and our Python code is accountable for this feat.

Let's say you're using a web service's API - perhaps a cloud-based financial data provider that requires OAuth for accessing its resources. With Python, you would typically go through the following steps:

- Register your application with the service. You'll get a client ID and a client secret.
- In your Python code, you'd ask for the user's authorization, redirecting them to another URL provided by the service.
- If the user authorizes the access, they're redirected back to your application with an authorization token.
- Your application exchanges this authorization token for an access token by making a POST request to the service.

In Python, you can use particular libraries like `requests` and `requests_oauthlib` to perform OAuth easily. It allows us to work with various OAuth flavors, including OAuth1 (sometimes used by older APIs) and OAuth2 (more common with modern APIs).

```python
from requests_oauthlib import OAuth2Session

# Define your client ID, client secret, and the URL you'll redirect
users to
```

```
client_id = 'your_client_id_here'
client_secret = 'your_client_secret_here'
redirect_uri = 'https://www.your_redirect_url.com'

# Define your authorization base and token URLs
auth_base_url = 'https://api.example.com/auth'
token_url = 'https://api.example.com/token'

# Create an OAuth2 Session
oauth = OAuth2Session(client_id, redirect_uri=redirect_uri)

# Get the authorization URL and state
auth_url, state = oauth.authorization_url(auth_base_url)

# Navigate to the authorization_url, authorize the app, and
you'll be redirected to the redirect_uri. The URL will contain an
authorization code.
# Extract auth_code and use it to fetch the access token.

auth_code = 'your_auth_code_here'

token = oauth.fetch_token(
        token_url,
        client_secret=client_secret,
        authorization_response=auth_code
        )
```

Once you have the access token, you can use it to make authorized API requests on behalf of the user.

Token-based authentication is a cornerstone of OAuth. However, it also finds use in another popular protocol — JSON Web Tokens (JWT). In JWT, a user verifying their identity with their credentials results in the server generating a unique encoded token. This token is returned to the user who stores it and includes it in all subsequent requests.

Taken together, OAuth and token-based authentication gulp the bitter authentication pill, making it digestible for programmers, and effectively bolt our data doors, ensuring our valuable financial data stays secure while being accessible for Python and Excel to work their magic.

In the thrilling lyrical drama of data interaction, OAuth and token-based authentication play their part exquisitely. They add the perfect encore to the symphony, casting enchantment, and ensuring a secure data flow. As our Python-Excel spectacle continues, let's cherish this piece of the puzzle that we've successfully unraveled, ready for the ensuing acts.

Mastering OAuth and Token-based authentication adds a rich note to our data symphony, paving the way for secure, smooth, and efficient data exchanges. As we conclude this discussion, reflecting on the insightful foray into the enchanting world of authentication, we acknowledge the critical role of these techniques in our Python-Excel journey. Let us march forward, armed with this newfound comprehension, eager to further unravel the complex, yet enchanting realm of data interaction, and continue scripting our unique composition in the grand Python-Excel concert.

Webhooks and Real-time Data

Webhooks, often referred to as 'reverse' APIs, are automated methods for applications to communicate with each other in near real-time. So, how exactly does this magic happen? The answer is delightfully simple and whispers of unparalleled elegance. When an event occurs in the source application – imagine a new piece of financial data being generated – it sends a HTTP POST payload to the webhook's configured URL. This notification prompts immediate action, initiating the breathtaking ballet of real-time data flow.

Now, let's extrapolate this to our realm, where financial data is constantly evolving and time sensitivity is key. Webhooks allow your Python code to listen for these events in real-time, thereby enabling it to retrieve, process, and guide this data into your Excel spreadsheets the moment it becomes available. Instead of a repetitive routine where your code continually polls the API server, webhooks metamorphose your data interaction into a responsive, event-driven dance. The silver lining? Optimised traffic, reduced latency, and the exhilarating promise of real-time data-processing.

To weave together the power of Python, Excel, and webhooks, we first need to configure our webhook URL, which will be the designated listener for the API server's notifications. Following this, we need Python code that can process the incoming HTTP POST requests. Flask, a lightweight Python web framework, is perfect for this task:

```python
from flask import Flask, request

app = Flask(__name__)
```

```
# Define the route that will respond to the webhook POST
request
@app.route('/webhook', methods=['POST'])
def respond():
    # Extract the JSON payload of the POST request
    payload = request.json

    # Process the received data suitably...
    process_data(payload)

    # Response for the API server to confirm successful receipt
    return {"message": "Data received and processed"}, 200
` ` `
```

Ideally, this server needs to be persistently running and accessible on the public internet for the API server to communicate with it. Deploying our Flask app on platforms like Heroku or AWS amplifies its power and readies it for the grand data symphony.

To fully appreciate the potential of this simple Flask application, imagine a financial trading system wherein stock prices are being updated in real-time. As soon as a specified stock hits a specific price, the data provider's API server sends a POST request to our application, which immediately processes the data and updates the relevant analytics in the Excel spreadsheet. Our model, thus armed with real-time data, can make informed, instantaneous decisions - the triumph of Python, Excel, and webhooks!

As we waltz in this exciting sphere of near real-time data interaction, we comprehend the power of webhooks and the utility they bring into our Python-Excel tableau. Greeting the API server's notifications with immediate action, our Python code, like a diligent conductor, takes the baton from webhooks and guides the financial data into Excel's cells rhythmically. The result? A glorious performance of real-time data processing, hitting high notes of efficiency, responsiveness, and ultimately, success.

Scraping Dynamic Websites

As our narrative of Python and Excel integration unravels further, we plunge into the more tumultuous waves of data extraction - scraping dynamic websites. Dynamic websites, with their stream of ever-changing content, can prove a formidable adversary. Yet, they are a treasure cove of fresh, relevant data that, when captured, can provide invaluable insights and make our Excel spreadsheets pulsate with life.

In contrast to static websites, rich with HTML for easy scraping, dynamic websites rely on JavaScript to load and display data; information often not accessible until a user action triggers it or after a waiting period. This idiosyncrasy, while enhancing user interaction, throws a wrench in the scraping process. Enter the world of Python libraries, like Selenium, Pyppeteer, and Scrapy, that allow us to triumph over this challenge and effectively scrape dynamic content.

One of the most commonly employed libraries for this task is Selenium, a powerful tool originally designed for automated testing of web applications, but serves equally well as a dynamic content web scraper. Selenium can interact with JavaScript, fill out forms, click buttons, and mimic other user behaviour that is often pivotal to revealing hidden data.

At its core, Selenium emulates a web browser allowing Python to control it programmatically and extract the required data. Here's a basic example showcasing how to load a dynamic website, interact with the JavaScript, and extract the resulting data:

```python
from selenium import webdriver

# Instantiate a Chrome browser (make sure Chromedriver is installed and in PATH)
driver = webdriver.Chrome()

# Open the dynamic page
driver.get('https://www.dynamicwebsite.com')

# Wait for the dynamic content to load or trigger the load by interacting with JavaScript
driver.implicitly_wait(10) # waits up to 10 seconds for elements to become available

# Extract the data
data_element = driver.find_element_by_id('dynamicData')
data = data_element.text

# Don't forget to close the browser!
driver.quit()
```

This simple Python script can unlock a world of dynamic content for your Excel spreadsheet. However, scraping dynamic websites is a wide ocean replete with varying undercurrents. While many tasks will be variations of this theme, deeper understanding, patience, and a knack for problem-solving will be your anchors when navigating through this more tumultuous end of the web scraping spectrum.

A word of caution, though. Web scraping imposes ethical and legal obligations. Respect website terms and conditions, and employ your new skills considering the privacy and rights of the website's maintainers and users. Always ensure you're authorised to scrape and use the data, and don't let your Python scripts hammer the website's servers. After all, with great power comes great responsibility.

Remember, every setback faced during this adventure is an opportunity to delve even deeper into the fascinating world of Python. As you conquer the shifting sands of dynamic website scraping, you bring back vital data, invaluable insights, enriched experience, and captured moments of gleaming triumph in the vast, seemingly daunting, terrain of web data extraction.

As we retreat from the uncharted waters of dynamic website scraping, we leave armed with enriched knowledge and a triumphant sense of accomplishment. Harnessing the power of Python and Selenium, we have broken the formidable barriers of dynamic content, adding a valuable weapon to our arsenal of data extraction tactics. By integrating this treasured data into our Excel spreadsheets, we not only breathe life into swathes of numbers but also set the stage for prudent and influential decision-making.

Thus, the endeavour of scraping dynamic websites becomes

less of a formidable adversary and more of a strategy-enriching adventure – a thrilling dive into the ocean of data. Concluding this part of our Python-Excel saga, we can look back at the waves traversed and the challenges conquered, all of which meticulously thread into the fabric of our growing mastery.

API Error Handling

APIs are the veins through which data flows in a digital environment. However, no network is immune to complications, and APIs are no exceptions. Errors can arise due to a multitude of issues and setting up error handling measures can help prevent these issues from stopping your scripts, alert you when they occur, or even correct them, maintaining the health of your Excel-driven applications.

Python has provided us with a robust set of tools to deal with errors and exceptions. The ubiquitous try-except block is often the cornerstone of error handling in Python.

```python
try:
    response = requests.get('https://api.someservice.com/v1/data')
    response.raise_for_status()
except requests.exceptions.HTTPError as err:
    print (f"HTTP error occurred: {err}")
except Exception as err:
    print (f"Other error occurred: {err}")
else:
```

```
    print("Data retrieved successfully!")
```
` ` `

In this code snippet, the Python script attempts to extract data from an API endpoint. The ` .raise_for_status()` function is called on the response, which will automatically throw an exception if the HTTP request returned an error code. This exception will be caught and handled, with the result being printed to the console. If no exception is caught, then the else clause will run and a success message will be printed.

This is a simple and adaptable illustration of handling API errors and exceptions. However, the world of APIs hosts a variety of errors like 502 - bad gateway, 503 - service unavailable, 429 - too many requests or even 404 - not found, and numerous others. Each of these errors narrates a different story and may require a unique approach to resolve.

For instance, a 429 error means that too many requests were sent in a given amount of time. This calls for introducing timeouts or rate limiting so as to not overwhelm the API server.

` ` `python
```
import time

for i in range(10):
    try:
        response = requests.get('https://api.someservice.com/
v1/data')
        response.raise_for_status()
    except requests.exceptions.HTTPError as err:
```

```
if response.status_code == 429:
    print("Rate limit exceeded. Waiting and retrying...")
    time.sleep(5)
else:
    print(f"HTTP error occurred: {err}")
except Exception as err:
    print(f"Other error occurred: {err}")
else:
    print("Data retrieved successfully!")
    break
```

In the above context, we add a loop for retrying the requests and introduce a wait period of 5 seconds if a 429 error is encountered. This is a simple illustration of rate limit handlers in API requests.

Dealing with errors in API communication is a vast field with countless potential complications. It's important to remember that Python exceptions are a deep and flexible system that can be leveraged to handle errors not only from APIs, but from any aspect of your program. Lastly, it's essential to keep in mind, reading and understanding the API documentation will always be the initial key to successfully navigating API territory.

Just like a well-executed act in the circus ring, API handling calls for a confluence of precision, understanding, and constant improvement. As we bid adieu to this topic, it's important to remember - the spotlight is on learning, growing, and evolving by acknowledging the fact that to err is not just human, but also, sometimes, APIs.

Ethical Considerations

APIs open the door to limitless possibilities. They allow us to interact with external services and leverage their functionalities without having to understand the underlying complexity. However, with great power comes great responsibility. Just because you can access data or use a service through an API, should you? This is where ethics come into play.

Just as in more general programming spheres, ethical considerations apply when dealing with APIs. Ethical use is especially important for publicly available APIs, where the potential for misuse is even greater.

Observing ethical considerations when using APIs can be distilled down to two primary areas - respecting the author's guidelines as described in the API documentation and respecting the data you have access to and its subsequent use.

When you access an API, you essentially enter into a contract with the API provider to use their resources in a way they deem acceptable. The API documentation functions as your guidebook, outlining how one should interact with the service. It specifies rate limits, data usage terms, and potential restrictions. Keeping within these guidelines isn't just legal - it's ethical.

Let's look at a simple Python script interacting with an API.

```python
import requests
```

```
response    =    requests.get('https://api.someservice.com/v1/
data')

data = response.json()

for record in data['records']:
    print(record['field_to_access'])
` ` `
```

Perhaps it's easy to assume that once we have obtained the data, we can use it as we please. However, using data mindlessly can lead to ethical concerns. Personal information of any kind carries heavy ethical implications. Even if the data isn't obviously personal, using it might still potentially disclose sensitive information.

API ethics is also about honouring the privacy and rights of the data subjects. This may extend from the nature of the data right down to how often you make requests to the server. Think of APIs as a shared resource, and when you're accessing public APIs, you are sharing them with countless other developers. Understanding the value of community resources and using them responsibly can make the world of APIs a better place.

Consistent with the values of respecting API's guidelines and the data you have access to is the consideration of the impact of your code. Whether you realise it or not, the code you write can have far-reaching effects, particularly when automating tasks with APIs. Used inappropriately, you could flood a site with traffic, drain system resources, or even accidentally deny service to other users. Applying foresight and care to the potential ramifications of your code isn't just good programming—it's ethical programming.

Realising that ethics is essentially about respect—for the service you are using, for the data you access, and for the wider community—can be the first step towards creating a thoughtful, ethical approach to API usage.

One must always bear in mind the ethical implications of their use of APIs. It's part of being a responsible, ethical programmer, enhancing the industry we work in and fostering trust in the technologies we so heavily depend on.

Creating, prototyping, launching, and distributing solutions involve a spectrum of ethical concerns, a veritable maze that requires navigation. As we journey through this labyrinth, learning and innovating, may our understanding of ethical considerations serve as the Ariadne's thread, guiding us and ensuring we don't lose our way.

CHAPTER 10: BUILDING CUSTOM PYTHON TOOLS FOR EXCEL

Introduction to Excel Add-ins

When considering the landscape of Excel programming, it is impossible to neglect the crucial component that has profoundly upped the game and empowered users worldwide - Excel Add-ins. Whether you are a seasoned whizz at Excel or a recent entrant into the landscape of Excel programming, the captivating world of Add-ins is something that can significantly enhance your Python for Excel prowess. In this chapter, we will be exploring this game-changing contribution deeper, understanding its integral significance and how to leverage it, paving the way for a seamless Excel-Python experience.

In Excel, Add-ins play a fundamentally important role. They are independent programs that plug into Excel to offer enhanced functionality. They can come pre-built with Excel, be developed by third parties or even custom-made using programming languages like Python or VBA.

Before we delve into the heart of Excel Add-ins, let's first understand why they are an essential element in the toolkit of every Excel enthusiast. Add-ins provide users with the capacity to enhance Excel's capacity drastically— be it introducing new functionality, streamlining workflow, or even automating routine tasks. They act as a bridge by bringing advanced features and time-saving functions into the Excel user interface.

The revolutionizing aspect of Add-ins is their ability to integrate programming disciplines within the Excel environment, not just VBA but also, our primary focus here, Python. Add-ins can contain Python scripts, allowing us to use Python's full capacity right within Excel.

To illustrate what an Add-in can do, consider the hypothetical task where you'll want to predict future cash flow based on historical data. In Python, it might involve analysing the data, modeling, and running algorithms. With the help of an Excel Add-in, all these can be done smoothly right within Excel's environment.

Creating an Excel Add-in using Python can be done with xlwings, a fantastic open-source library. It allows us to integrate Python scripts, creating user-defined functions and interacting with Excel sheets using Python in real time. Here is a simple example showing how this works:

```python
import xlwings as xw

def hello_xlwings():
    wb = xw.Book.caller() # creates a reference to the calling
```

Excel file

```
sheet = wb.sheets[0]

sheet["A1"].value = "Hello, xlwings!" # inserts our message
into cell A1
```
` ` `

This is only an introduction to what Python Add-ins can do. Consider more complex circumstances, where extensive data manipulations, machine learning model creation, analyzing large volumes of data, or complex data visualizations are needed. In those instances, programming Excel with Python Add-ins can offer limitless possibilities and significant time savings.

So, are Add-ins just for Python programmers looking to have more fun with Excel? Not at all! They are also incredible solutions for less tech-savvy users needing to perform complex tasks. Pre-built Add-ins can be distributed to these users, enabling them to function at higher effectiveness levels. This corresponds not only to businesses and organizations but also to less-tech-savvy individuals who can harness the immense potential Add-ins offer without knowing how to program.

Add-ins infuse the dynamic energy of syntax languages into a static grid of cells, converting the mundane into the extraordinary. Whether it's data analysis infused with machine learning or automating repetitive tasks, Excel add-ins provide a touch of elegance, making your operations smooth and impressively efficient.

The vision of embedding Python functionality into the user-friendly environment of Excel is surely revolutionary, opening up endless possibilities of application, innovation, and performance efficiency. Embedded in this game-changing insight is also a momentous challenge of mastering this indispensable toolset that can propel your Excel journey to new heights. So buckle up for this exciting expedition to revolutionize your Excel operations with the power of add-ins, as each subsequent chapter takes you deeper down this enchanting rabbit hole. Remember, the magic of Excel awaits and it starts with Excel add-ins!

Creating a Custom Ribbon

Imagine, for a moment, having an Excel navigational interface precisely tuned to cater to your distinct application needs. A dynamic landscape of functionalities, commands, and actions aligned to your interactive routine, saving you precious time, and improving application efficiency. Enter the realm of custom ribbons, ancillary interfaces enabling users to personalise Excel's environment to their preference.

In the next segments of this chapter, we will understand the fascinating concept of custom ribbon creation and how it takes personalisation to novel heights. We will explore the underlying principles of custom ribbons, discover the process of designing one, and the incorporation of Python functionality to create a thoroughly customised, efficient, and user-centred Excel experience.

The concept of a customised ribbon is straightforward and captivating. Suppose you routinely use a specific set of functions across different Excel tabs or commonly execute several tasks using VBA or Python. In that case, a custom ribbon can give you instant access to these commands, saving you hours of navigation and selection time.

Creating a custom ribbon with Python and VBA can be highly beneficial. Not only does it offer a user-defined set of commands and actions readily available, but it can also harbor Python scripts executed directly from the ribbon, making Excel programming seamless and intuitive.

To create a custom ribbon with Python, we can use libraries like `pyvsto` that allow for custom ribbon creation. However, it might require an understanding of XML as Microsoft's Ribbon interface uses it.

A more straightforward way could be using Excel's inbuilt Ribbon customization features. To demonstrate, let's create a VBA function and call it from our custom Ribbon:

1. In Excel, click the Ribbon's right-click and choose 'Customize the Ribbon'.

2. In the new window, you can create a new Tab and add a new command to it.

3. In the Macro selection, you can pick the VBA function you want to associate with it.

```vb
Sub MyCustomFunction()
    MsgBox "My custom function executed!"
End Sub
```

While VBA allows for creating a custom Ribbon user-interface, to bring the strength of Python into the mix, you'll need to use tools like xlwings to call Python from VBA. Here's how:

```vb
Sub RunPythonScript()

    RunPython ("import my_python_script; my_python_script.run()")

End Sub
```

In the example above, your `my_python_script.py` file should be in the same directory as your Excel workbook. And you would have a function named `run()` in your `my_python_script.py` file.

By combining Excel's Ribbon customization feature with the ability to call Python from Excel, you can create a truly customised Excel-Python development environment. By creating buttons and commands that directly call your Python scripts, you can automate tasks, perform complex calculations, or even plot advance visualizations, all from your custom Ribbon.

To fully harness the power of Python, you can build Python Add-ins with libraries like xlwings and associate them with your custom Ribbon, allowing for a more rich user interface and scripts execution available directly on Excel's interface.

The Ribbon Renaissance: Excel Personalisation for Enhanced Efficiency

As our exploration of the world of custom ribbons concludes, we can confidently put forth that customising the Ribbon interface forms an essential cog in the Python-Excel integration. The Ribbon is not just an ordinary interface. It is the battleground where data fights for understanding and transformation. It is where Excel's aesthetics meet Python's logic and where routine meets automation.

When augmented with the power of Python, custom ribbons aren't just a plain row of buttons and commands. They transform into dynamic tool strips that breathe your programming paradigms into Excel, providing instant script execution, access to complex functionalities, and above all, an environment tuned to your preference.

The vision of customising Excel's ever-familiar interface to users' unique needs is a profound one. It opens unprecedented conveniences and interaction possibilities, enhancing user efficiency and reducing task execution time significantly. Mapping this nuanced interaction blueprint onto Excel's interface is an exceptional way to extend Python's power within the Excel environment and make it more user-friendly.

Suffice to say, the quest to harness Excel's full potential would be incomplete devoid of the intuitive elegance of customised ribbons. So, as we navigate further into the ocean of Python-Excel integration, let's carry along with this tool, a keystroke away, yet powerful enough to revolutionise your Excel experience.

Building Excel Functions with Python

If you've ever yearned for custom Excel functions that behave precisely as you need them to, consider this your lucky day! Python, with its versatility and power, allows us to create bespoke functions in Excel. From complex financial models to comprehensive data analytics algorithms, this feature unlocks a new world of functionality within the otherwise restrictive

Excel function palette.

In this section, let's delve deeper into the fascinating world of Excel functions powered by Python. We'll show you how to build your own Python-powered Excel functions, contributing your unique insights to Excel computation.

Excel, on its own, carries an impressive array of pre-existing functions. However, the real magic begins when we start creating tailor-made functionalities in Excel using Python. This approach brings Python's immensity and adaptability into Excel, enhancing your spreadsheet tasks with Python's superior computational capabilities and ease of use.

Let's start with some basics. Our goal here is to create a User Defined Function (UDF) in Excel using Python. UDFs in Excel are nothing more than custom functions that can behave like any built-in function.

To achieve this, we need to utilise Python libraries that provide a user-friendly interface for integrating Python with Excel; one of them is `xlwings`.

`xlwings` is a Python library that makes the integration of Excel with Python a breeze. Among its strengths is the ability to write UDFs in Python and use them in Excel. The Python functions are exposed to Excel through a simple decorator. Here's a basic example:

```python
import xlwings as xw

@xw.func
```

```python
def greet(name):
    return f"Hello, {name}!"
```

Now the `greet` function can be called directly from an Excel cell, like any built-in Excel function: `=greet(A1)`

The `@xw.func` decorator is critical; it tells `xlwings` to treat the function as a UDF.

Now that we have a basic grip of how we can define a UDF with `xlwings`, let's up the ante. Suppose we need a function that fetches and processes data from a web API, another instance where Python trumpets Excel's built-in capabilities.

```python
import requests
import xlwings as xw

@xw.func
def fetch_data(url):
    response = requests.get(url)
    data = response.json()

    # Process the data in some way
    processed_data = ...

    return processed_data
```

In the example above, we used `requests` library to fetch data from a web API, something that's not directly possible in Excel.

Python UDFs aren't just confined to returning simple data types. We can return complex data structures like lists and arrays, and `xlwings` will conveniently write them to Excel as ranges. You could easily return an entire dataset from an API endpoint with a single custom function in Excel, drastically reducing the time needed to manually import and process data.

Creating Excel functions with Python will expand your Excel horizon and how you interact with spreadsheets. It provides a new level of customization, streamlines complex processes, and incorporates complex external functionalities.

So, here we are, at the confluence of Python's simplicity and Excel's universality. We have learnt that Python doesn't just interact with Excel—it moulds, shapes, and extends it. By creating Excel functions powered by Python, we're not simply using another library or tool; we're evolving with Excel, progressing from users to architects, dictating how we utilize and interact with it.

To conclude, UDFs in Python bring an unparalleled depth of customization and sophistication to our Excel workbooks. These functions break Excel's built-in limitations, pushing boundaries, and opening a new world of spreadsheet computation. Armed with UDFs, we can blend Python's computational prowess with Excel's interface familiarity, creating advanced models, automate repetitive tasks, or fetch and process data from external sources.

User Authentication and Authorization

The necessity for security is gigantic and unavoidable in today's digital realm. Whether it's a simple Excel add-in or a complex, multifaceted application, User Authentication and Authorization are two of the most fundamental elements of any secure system. It's time to bring our understanding of Python and Excel to the fore and witness the magic they create in maintaining the formidable bastion of security.

When it comes to establishing secure environments and safeguarding data, user authentication and authorization are paramount. Authentication verifies the identity of users before providing access, while authorization determines which resources and actions the authenticated user can access.

As creators of Excel add-ins leveraging Python's power, we have access to a number of effective libraries to integrate these essential functions, such as `OAuthLib`.

Authentication:

`OAuthLib` is a Python library that provides a simple capability to implement OAuth, a widely used protocol for secure API authentication. Google APIs, for example, use OAuth 2.0.

We'll start by creating an OAuth 2.0 flow that guides us through the process of authenticating the user:

```python
```

```python
from oauthlib.oauth2 import BackendApplicationClient
from requests_oauthlib import OAuth2Session

def authenticate(client_id, client_secret):
    client = BackendApplicationClient(client_id=client_id)
    oauth = OAuth2Session(client=client)
    token = oauth.fetch_token(token_url='https://provider.com/oauth2/token', client_id=client_id,
                client_secret=client_secret)
    return token
```

With this function, you can authenticate your application with the API provider and retrieve an access token. You can then use this token to make authenticated requests on behalf of the user.

Authorization:

With authentication in place, we need to ensure that users can only access what they are entitled to. This is where the concept of authorization comes in. Each user role must be given different permissions to perform various actions.

In Python, `flask_principal` is a very useful library for managing roles and permissions. Let's assume we have three types of user roles - Admin, Editor, Viewer. We can set up these roles and their permissions using the `flask_principal` library like so:

```python
```

```python
from flask_principal import RoleNeed, Permission

admin_permission = Permission(RoleNeed('admin'))
editor_permission = Permission(RoleNeed('editor'))
viewer_permission = Permission(RoleNeed('viewer'))
```

Once the permissions are set according to the roles, we can add them to the routes or functions in the application:

```python
@app.route('/edit')
@admin_permission.require(http_exception=403)
def edit():
    return 'Only Admin can see this!'
```

While these are just the basics, the depth of user authentication and authorization is vast and depends on the complexity of the system. You can implement multi-factor authentication, biometric authentication, and even blockchain-based authentication. Similarly, sophisticated systems can have role-based, attribute-based, or policy-based authorization mechanisms.

Remember, security is never a one-time thing; it's not something that you can just set up and forget. It's an ongoing process that requires constant vigilance and adaptations to handle ever-evolving threats.

Through the amalgamation of Python's robust libraries

and Excel's wide applicability, we've successfully navigated the maze of user authentication and authorization—two essentials in strengthening your Excel add-ins against unauthorised access.

To summarise, authentication and authorization form the bedrock of user security in any digital system. Incorporating these in your Excel add-ins not only safeguards sensitive data but also enhances user trust in your application's integrity.

Remember: Developing software isn't just about the features it can offer, but also the security it provides. While Python and Excel provide you with the tools to create brilliant applications, they also empower you with the capability to make those applications secure.

As we continue unravelling the potential of integrating Python with Excel, let's ensure to keep security at the forefront. With Python's rich support for secure programming and Excel's flexible user interface, you can provide both functionality and safety—making your Excel add-ins shine in the world of advanced spreadsheet computation.

Packaging and Distribution

In an ever-connected world, potential users of your Excel add-ins could span the globe. It's important then to understand and perfect the last but vastly critical stage in the creation of any software solution: packaging and distribution. This segment will walk you through how to bundle your Python and Excel innovations effectively and ensure they reach your international audience intact and ready to use.

To enable other users to enjoy the fruits of your labour

(your unique Python-powered Excel add-ins), you need to meticulously package your software for distribution and ensure it's easily installable and executable on their systems.

A well-thought manual helps users understand how to employ your add-in to maximum effect. Beyond descriptive text, Python's sphinx utility can compile readable and neat HTML or PDF files.

For distributing your code, Python provides several tools such as `setup.py`, `pip` and `PyPI`.

Creating a `setup.py` script for your project makes it easier for users to install. This script includes project metadata like name, version, description and what Python versions it supports.

A basic `setup.py` file might look something similar to this:

```python
from setuptools import setup, find_packages

setup(
    name='Your Addin',
    version='1.0.0',
    long_description=__doc__,
    packages=find_packages(),
    include_package_data=True,
    zip_safe=False,
    install_requires=[
        'Flask'
```

```
    ],
)
```

The `install_requires` parameter lists all the Python dependencies of your project to ensure they are installed along with your software.

To facilitate easy installation, package your Python application into an executable file. PyInstaller is a notable tool for this, simplifying the process with command-line functions:

```shell
pyinstaller your-program.py
```

PyInstaller supports numerous libraries, making it a fantastic choice for Python-driven Excel add-ins.

Distributing Your Add-in:

Usually, you would distribute your software through a centralised platform where users could download the necessary executable or installation files. However, Python also offers the Python Package Index (PyPI) - a central repository of Python software anyone can contribute to.

To distribute your Python code, package and upload it to PyPI:

```shell
python setup.py sdist bdist_wheel
twine upload dist/*
```

` ` `

After this, anyone can install your package using pip, Python's package installer:

` ` ` shell

pip install your-package

` ` `

Consider including a detailed README file and comprehensive documentation with your package. They should be explicit about installation steps and requirements to ensure users have a smooth experience.

Integration with Excel:

Finally, remember that your Python-powered Excel add-ins must fit seamlessly into Excel. Instructions regarding the installation and use of your Excel add-ins should be detailed within an Excel interface (like 'Help' pages). You may utilize Excel's Ribbon feature to neatly package your add-in features and offer users an intuitive and professional interface for your proprietary tools.

In a nutshell, the end-game is to craft a carefully packaged Python application and Excel add-in that is easy for your end-users to install and use.

The crux of the matter is simple: developing an innovative Excel add-in is an accomplishment, but for it to reach its potential, packaging and distribution are critical. As we've seen, Python offers us a bounty of tools to package our project efficiently and effectively.

Relieving your users from complex installations and

configurations means they can dive right into the game-changing functionalities you've incorporated into Excel, making their computational tasks swift, automated, and error-free.

Packaging and distributing your Python Excel add-in in a user-friendly manner will increase adoption, improve customer satisfaction, and create a positive atmosphere around your product. It is the foundation upon which the tower of your success stands, visible from afar and reaching out for the stars.

Remember, the better your software is packaged and easier it is to install, the more likely it is to be widely used and valued. So, let's continue this journey of Python and Excel, taking these powerful tools to the masses, democratizing computations one spreadsheet at a time.

User Interface Design Principles

Crafting an elegant, user-friendly interface for your Python Excel add-ins is as important as developing the functionality itself. A well-designed interface is intuitive, efficient, and enhances your user's experience as they interact with your add-in. In this segment, we open a window to the wide world of interface design principles that lead to a user-centric Excel add-in.

Every system, be it computer software or physical machinery, strives for one goal: usability. In this digital era, where software solutions abound, users don't just want a functional tool; they want one that is easy to use.

Your Python for Excel add-ins is no exception. In the shadows of Python's logical brilliance, Excel's user interface basks in the sunlight. Your task is to blend these worlds seamlessly, enhancing usability and delighting customers.

Achieving such a superior user interface (UI) requires a mastery of design principles. Let's delve into this fascinating sphere to grasp its core:

Clarity:

Clear, understandable interfaces win the day. Avoid overly complex elements. Keep your interface easy, clean, and consistent. The UI should communicate the purpose of each element visually. Take advantage of Excel's pre-existing interface elements as a guide and create elements that enhance the existing style and theme.

Familiarity:

Users come with certain preconceptions about how things should work. Leverage this familiarity. Users shouldn't feel like they're exploring a new universe every time they use your add-in.

Responsiveness:

A good UI communicates to the user what's happening at all times. If a process will take time, communicate that to the user, potentially using a progress bar or spinner.

Consistency:

Familiarity is reinforced by consistency. Consistent designs are easy to learn and navigate. Maintain uniformity with button designs, terminologies, colour schemes, and workflows.

Efficiency:

The UI should not be a barrier to productivity. It should be designed to minimize user input. Automate repetitive tasks, provide keyboard shortcuts, and quick access buttons for commonly used features.

Flexibility and Customizability:

Allow users to customize the interface to suit their needs. This creates emotional ownership and increases user satisfaction. The genius lies in balancing the flexibility of customization with clarity and efficiency of default settings.

Error Prevention and Recovery:

Errors are occasional unwanted guests. Minimize the chances of user error by careful UI design. Whenever an error does occur, it should be easy for the user to understand and recover from it.

Affordance and feedback:

Every UI element should intuitively hint at its functionality, a feature known as affordance. Additionally, users should receive instantaneous feedback on their interactions, informing them about the outcome of their actions.

Accessibility:

Accessibility should be factored into every aspect of your design. Make sure your add-in is usable by everyone, including those with visual or other impairments.

A snippet of the design process could involve adding a dropdown menu to your add-in in Excel:

```python
import xlwings as xw
import functools

@xw.func
def make_dropdown(cell="A1", options=['Yes', 'No']):
    validation = cell.api.validation
    validation.add(3,3,1,1)
    validation.InputTitle = 'My dropdown'
    validation.ErrorTitle = 'An error occurred'
    validation.InputMessage = 'Please select an option.'
    validation.ErrorMessage = 'Your selection is not in the list.'
    validation.IgnoreBlank = True
    validation.InCellDropdown = True
    validation.Formula1 = ",".join(options)
```

This decrease the chances of input errors by limiting user options to a predefined list, an excellent example of both clarity and error prevention.

Designing an excellent interface for your Python Excel add-in goes beyond reducing user effort and improving the overall experience. Here lies the craft of turning the complex simple, bridging the gap between your add-ins' powerful features and end-users.

The interface isn't merely a necessary feature; it's the face of your Python Excel add-in—the first point of contact with the user. A well-designed interface will not just empower your users but impress them, enhancing their overall interaction and leaving them eager to explore further.

After all, Python and Excel together are a power-packed combination, but without a thoughtful user interface, it's like a finely tuned engine hidden under an uninviting hood. Let's make your Excel add-ins a joy to use, and an instrumental part of spreading the love of Python in the world of Excel, one user-friendly interface at a time.

Advanced Custom Objects and Form Controls

Custom objects and advanced form controls are staples in the realm of UI design. They are featured prominently in high-performing applications - and for good reason. They offer an additional layer of flexibility and sophistication that makes your Excel add-ins not just functional, but engaging and intuitive.

Custom Objects – The Freedom of Expression:

In Python, objects encapsulate data with functions operating on that data. Coupled with its class feature, Python offers the ability to create your custom object types. Excel add-ins require interaction with a wide array of data types, wherein the versatility of custom objects truly shines.

Let's imagine you're creating an add-in for a sales team. They deal with customers, each represented by a flurry of data: name, contacts, preferences, sales history, target sales, etc. Instead of treating these as separate data points, Python allows you to bundle these into a custom object – say, a "Customer" object. This simplifies data management and enhances code readability.

Moreover, linking this object with relevant methods, such as 'calculateLifetimeValue' or 'displayPurchaseHistory', makes data processing smoother and more intuitive.

```python
class Customer:
    def __init__(self, name, contacts, preferences, sales_history, target_sales):
        self.name = name
        self.contacts = contacts
        self.preferences = preferences
        self.sales_history = sales_history
        self.target_sales = target_sales

    def calculateLifetimeValue(self):
        # Function for calculating Lifetime Value
        pass

    def displayPurchaseHistory(self):
        # Function to display purchase history
        pass
```

Form Controls - The Unsung Heroes:

Form controls are the unsung heroes of interactive Excel. They comprise elements like buttons, checkboxes, radio buttons, drop-down lists, etc., driving user interaction and controlling how users input data.

While Python for Excel shines through automated tasks and data manipulation, form controls bring a much-coveted interactive angle. For instance, a simple button can initiate a complex Python script in the background, while an alarmingly red checkbox could reflect a threshold breach in real time.

Talk about conjuring power from simplicity!

Going a notch higher, advanced form controls bring magic into mundane Excel activities. Think of list boxes that auto populate based on user input, or scroll bars that adjust thousands of rows of data with a slight nudge.

Take an investment portfolio analysis tool, for instance. Instead of manually inputting asset weights, users could work with a series of slider controls synced with Python code. Adjusting the slider adjusts the asset weight, dynamically updating the return, risk, and other parameters. A complex task transformed into a fun, interactive experience.

```python
@xw.sub
def sliderChange():
    sht = xw.Book.caller().sheets['Sheet1']
    slider = sht.api.Slider1
```

```
weight = slider.Value / 100

# Rest of the code interacting with Python financial models,
etc.
```
` ` `

Beautiful isn't it? An advanced form control code snippet that could change the face of Excel interaction.

Creating Python Excel add-ins has been quite the journey. From understanding Python's nuances to tapping Excel's potential, the path has been exciting and informative. As you immerse yourself in advanced custom objects and form controls, you are scripting an Excel transformation.

Keep in mind, your creativity is the only limit when creating custom objects - design these to meticulously address the issues your add-in is solving. Build advanced form controls that are not only practical and coherent but also engaging and expressive. The amalgamation of these pioneering facets makes your add-in not just a tool, but more of a personalised experience for its users.

Your Python journey intertwined with Excel pivots at the understanding of these subtle yet powerful facets. Custom objects and advanced form controls, once mastered, will make your add-ins exceed expectations, becoming a benchmark of quality and ingenuity. And in this grand scheme, the user stands front and central.

CHAPTER 11:
CASE STUDIES
AND REAL-WORLD
APPLICATIONS

Financial Data Analysis
and Forecasting

The growth of a tree requires not just deep-rooted seeds and nourished soil, but also careful propagation. Translating this analogy to our journey in Python Excel Add-ins, we have equipped ourselves with Python Essentials and Excel Integration. We have nourished ourselves with Advanced Custom Objects and Form Controls. Now comes the final flourish of propagation - the packaging and distribution of our Python Excel Add-ins.

Think of packaging as the elegant, high-end casing around the luxurious, high-performance engine we've just built; a layer of polish to make our add-ins not just functional, but also attractive and user-friendly.

Python offers a series of modules, such as setuptools, py2exe, PyInstaller, among others, to package your code into standalone executables or libraries. These allow your add-ins to be independent of a Python installation, adding a layer of convenience for users not well-versed in Python.

A critical part of packaging is including dependencies – the modules and libraries your code relies on. Python's virtual environments add a degree of robustness here by isolating dependencies, ensuring version compatibility, and reducing conflicts with other Python projects.

Below is a simple setup.py file using setuptools:

```python
from setuptools import setup

setup(
    name="Python_Excel_Addin",
    version="0.1",
    scripts=["addin.py"],
    install_requires=[
        "xlwings", "numpy", "pandas", "matplotlib"
    ]
)
```

This file describes your add-in and its dependencies clearly. Running 'python setup.py install' from a command line installs the add-in with all prerequisites onto the system's Python environment.

Distribution - Taking it to the World

Distribution is the following step of making your Python Excel add-ins reach the ends of the globe. It offers the ease of use your sophisticated code deserves and grants it the exposure it needs.

Modules like distutils and setuptools simplify the distribution process by creating platform-specific executables or "distributable" Python archives. For example, here's how setuptools can transform our packaged add-in to a distributable .tar.gz file:

```python
python setup.py sdist
```

This singular line generates a source distribution, ready for usage or further distribution via channels like the Python Package Index (PyPI).

Surprisingly, Excel itself can serve as a carrier of Python add-ins. By connecting the add-in to Excel templates (.xlsm files) bearing the Python scripts, you can distribute these templates among users, equipping them with the power of Python right in their Excel environment!

Taking the deployment a notch higher, cloud services like AWS or Microsoft Azure can host your add-ins and provide APIs to directly enable Excel-Python interaction.

```python
@xw.func
def myFunction(input_value):
```

```
result = performCalculation(input_value)

return result

` ` `
```

The xw.func decorator marks myFunction() as callable from Excel. Once your Excel file has been exposed as a REST API, this function can be invoked from anywhere.

Remember, the smoother the user experience in installing and using your add-ins, the more usage (and recognition) they garner.

The world of Python and Excel is a vast expanse. By crafting a comprehensive understanding of Packaging and Distribution, you're ready to reshape this landscape with your Python Excel add-ins.

Every well-packaged and wisely distributed add-in brings us closer to that perfect symphony of Python's robustness and Excel's simplicity. So, as you embark on this phase, remember, the ease with which you can encapsulate Python's capabilities and expose them to Excel users enriches not just their experience but also widens Python's usability in the dynamic environment of Excel.

Dynamic Reporting and Visualization

The user interface (UI) is the gateway through which users interact with our Python Excel Add-ins. Thus, it becomes intrinsic for us to craft a user interface that is not just functional, but also visually pleasing, intuitive, and efficient.

User Interface design principles serve as the compass guiding us towards creating an enriching user experience. Here, we discuss the key principles while designing an optimal UI for your Python Excel Add-Ins.

Consistency is Key

The principle of consistency follows the mantra, "More of the same". A coherent design language with consistent elements, layout and aesthetic makes the application more predictable, enhancing the user's comfort level. In Python, wxPython is a popular choice for maintaining consistent UI elements across different Operating Systems while creating TKinter GUIs.

Make it Intuitive

The best interface is the one where users know how to navigate effortlessly. It's like walking into a library - You intuitively know where to find what you're looking for. Python's Tkinter library can help in creating intuitive drag and drop interfaces with the tkDnD module.

Less is More

The principle of simplicity suggests eliminating unnecessary elements that don't support user tasks. Providing clarity and simplicity while building Python Excel add-ins is a significant user interface design principle. KISS ("Keep It Simple, Stupid") should be your go-to strategy here. Design your GUIs with only the most essential elements, reducing clutter and confusion, resulting in a streamlined user interface.

Feedback Matters

Feedback provides users with an acknowledgment of their

actions giving users a sense of control and satisfaction. Python's rich set of libraries can help us implement vibrant feedback mechanisms, be it through a simple print statement or complex GUI pop-ups. For example, the tkinter.messagebox can be used to display feedback in a simple dialog window.

Placement and Hierarchical Organization

Controls that are used together should be grouped together. The Fitt's law from human-computer interaction can be an instrumental guide here implying that the size and distance of the target affect the time it takes to move the cursor to it. Therefore, frequently used controls and buttons should be centred and larger.

A considerable portion of Python's power in UI design comes from its libraries, like Tkinter, wxPython, PyQt, among others. For instance, creating a simple data entry form with validation is a breeze with Tkinter:

```python
from tkinter import *
from tkinter import messagebox

def validate_entry():
    if len(entry.get()) == 0:
        messagebox.showinfo("Error", "Please enter a value")

app = Tk()
entry = Entry(app)
entry.pack()
button            =           Button(app,          text="Validate",
```

```
command=validate_entry)
button.pack()
app.mainloop()
` ` `
```

In this example, clicking the "Validate" button triggers the "validate_entry" function which pops up a message box if the entry field is empty. This simple form of UI feedback helps users understand where they might have gone wrong.

Framing Interactions: Leveraging User Interface Design for Enhanced User Experience

In conclusion, an engaging, efficient and intuitive User Interface is a potent tool to enhance the user experience, drive user adoption and ultimately, make your Python Excel Add-in a rousing success. By understanding and implementing these key principles, you can create an inventive, user-oriented UI that brings your ideas alive.

Dynamic Reporting and Visualization form the golden thread that weaves through the fabric of any business decision-making process. Going beyond static spreadsheets and reports, we will now embark on the visually fascinating and intellectually stimulating world of dynamic reporting and visualization using Python and Excel.

Dynamic Reporting refers to reports that are interactive, allowing users to manipulate the views, filters, and drill down into the specifics. Python can interact seamlessly with Excel to generate these dynamic reports that enhance data consumption and decision making.

Python's wide array of packages like pandas, numpy, and

matplotlib, and Excel data slicers come together to deliver dynamic reports that are more than just a flat display of numbers. With data slicers in Excel and Python libraries, slicing and dicing through layers of data becomes a simple yet powerful exercise.

Visualization, on the other hand, is the art and science of telling stories with data. Just like an artist uses a palette of colours, we can use libraries such as pandas, seaborn, matplotlib, and plotly to bring data to life.

Using Python in conjunction with Excel's charting features can create a compelling visual narrative. You get the best of both worlds–Excel's wide variety of charts and Python's powerful data handling and additional plotting capabilities.

Here's a simple example of creating a dynamic bar plot using Python's matplotlib and Excel data:

```python
import pandas as pd
import matplotlib.pyplot as plt

# Load excel data using pandas
data = pd.read_excel("sales_data.xlsx")

# Create a dynamic bar plot
plt.bar(data["month"], data["sales"])
plt.title("Sales Data")
plt.xlabel("Month")
plt.ylabel("Sales")
```

plt.show()

` ` `

This script reads sales data from an Excel file and creates a simple dynamic bar plot. Changes in sales_data.xlsx reflect in the graph when the script runs, allowing for dynamic reporting.

Remember, a picture is worth a thousand cells. Visualization is not just about presenting data; it's about highlighting insights, spotting trends, and understanding patterns. It's about communicating complex data in a manner that is easy to comprehend.

Using Python and Excel together in this domain maps out a path to a more informed decision-making process, influencing strategy, operations, and everything in between.

The fusion of Python's analytical prowess and Excel's intuitive interface brings an unprecedented dynamism to our data storytelling capabilities. As we journey further in this realm of dynamic reporting and visualization, let's continue to leverage the power of Python with Excel to convert raw data into meaningful insights, helping your organization to navigate through this ocean of data, weathering all storms, and guiding you to your desired beacon of success.

Inventory Management

In the realm of business operations, inventory management stands as a critical function, impacting everything from customer satisfaction to the company's bottom line. As we journey into this chapter, we aim to harness the power of Python and Excel to redefine traditional inventory management processes, moving beyond simple spreadsheets towards strategic, data-driven decision making.

At its core, effective inventory management ensures that your businesses have the right amount of stock, at the right time. Whilst Excel has always been a popular tool for inventory management because of its accessibility and simplicity, when combined with Python, it becomes an even more potent tool capable of automated, scalable, and complex inventory management solutions.

Indeed, Python-Excel fusion can be effectively used to manage various facets of inventory operations, including inventory tracking, forecasting, replenishment, and reporting.

Python programs can pull in real-time data from various inventory management systems and databases, process it and populate Excel spreadsheets dynamically. Based on these dynamic spreadsheet data feeds, dashboards can be created in Excel for visual tracking and real-time monitoring of inventory levels.

Forecasting

Python's libraries like pandas, numpy, and sklearn can perform time-series analysis or use machine learning algorithms to predict future inventory needs. These forecasts can be pushed to Excel where decision-makers can interpret and use the data to make informed purchasing decisions.

For example, an ARIMA model (Autoregressive Integrated Moving Average), a widely used statistical method for time series forecasting, could be implemented in Python with the Statsmodels library to estimate future demand levels.

```python
import pandas as pd
from statsmodels.tsa.arima_model import ARIMA

# Import data
inventory_df = pd.read_excel('inventory_data.xlsx')

# Fit model
model = ARIMA(inventory_df['demand'], order=(5,1,0))
model_fit = model.fit(disp=0)

# Forecast
forecast, stderr, conf_int = model_fit.forecast(30) # 30-period forecast
```

Replenishment

Once forecasts are set, Python can also help define replenishment rules. For instance, 'Order Point/Order Quantity' rules can be established where if inventory drops to a certain level, an order for a predefined quantity is placed. These rules can be implemented in Python, which then dynamically updates the Excel tracking and reporting frameworks.

Dynamic Reporting

Python can generate dynamic reports by integrating, cleaning, and transforming data from different sources. These reports could include inventory trends, product performance, supplier reliability and so on. Combined with Excel's data visualization tools, they can help create an interactive, dynamic reporting environment.

```python
import pandas as pd

# Import data
data = pd.read_excel('sales_data.xlsx')

# Create a pivot table for the report
report = pd.pivot_table(data, values='Quantity', index=['Product'],
                columns='Month', aggfunc='sum', fill_value=0)

# Export the report to Excel
report.to_excel("report.xlsx")
```

This Python script reads sales data, creates a pivot table report with monthly sales quantity per product, and exports it back to Excel.

Social Media Analytics

As we delve into the plethora of opportunities offered by social media data for businesses, Python and Excel emerge as indispensable tools to unearth insights from the rivers of information flowing through platforms like Facebook, Twitter, Instagram, and LinkedIn. This chapter will guide you through the intricate web of social media analytics using Python's data extraction powers combined with Excel's intuitive interface.

Social media has evolved beyond socializing and has emerged as an invaluable business tool. With the number of individuals active on these platforms growing every day, social media hosts vast reserves of data ripe for analysis. Python, with its powerful libraries, provides the prowess needed to dissect and understand this data while Excel lends its user-friendly features for presenting and analyzing the parsed data.

Data Extraction and Cleaning

Python, with libraries such as Tweepy for Twitter, provides direct access to social media APIs, enabling you to extract real-time data based on specific parameters.

```python
import tweepy

# Replace these keys and tokens with your own!
consumer_key = "your_key"
consumer_secret = "your_secret"
access_token = "your_token"
access_token_secret = "your_token_secret"

auth = tweepy.OAuthHandler(consumer_key, consumer_secret)
auth.set_access_token(access_token, access_token_secret)

api = tweepy.API(auth)
```

```python
public_tweets = api.home_timeline(count=100) #fetches the 100 most recent tweets
for tweet in public_tweets:
    print(tweet.text)
```

When stored in Excel, you have a practical format for further analysis.

Sentiment Analysis

Python's text processing libraries, like NLTK or TextBlob, can be used to analyze the sentiment of social media posts and comments.

```python
from textblob import TextBlob

tweet = "your_tweet"
analysis = TextBlob(tweet)

if analysis.sentiment.polarity > 0:
    print('Positive')
elif analysis.sentiment.polarity == 0:
    print('Neutral')
else:
    print('Negative')
```

This information, when compiled in Excel, can help track the public's sentiment towards certain topics or brands.

Content Analytics

Content analytics can reveal patterns and trends in the topics that are most talked about. We can use Python's word processing libraries to analyze tweet content, after which Excel can be used to sort and visualize this data.

Reporting and Visualizations

Python's data analysis libraries can do everything from calculating simple statistics to running complex neural networks. Once analyzed, Excel's robust graphing and charting options help in visualizing this data.

```python
import pandas as pd

# Import data
data = pd.read_excel('Twitter_Data.xlsx')

# Create a pivot table for the report
report = pd.pivot_table(data, values='Likes', index=['Username'],
                columns='Month', aggfunc='sum', fill_value=0)

# Export the report to Excel
report.to_excel("report.xlsx")
```

As this Python script reads Twitter data, illustrates a pivot table report with monthly likes per username, and exports it back to Excel.

Health Data Management

A new epoch in healthcare is heralded as Python and Excel come together to revolutionize health data management. As healthcare sectors worldwide continue to amass astronomical amounts of data, there is an ever-pressure demand for competently handling, analyzing, and translating this data into actionable insights. In this chapter, we embark on an exploratory journey to unlock the potential of Python's sophisticated data handling capabilities coupled with Excel's analytical prowess for efficient and effective health data management.

The healthcare industry stands at the cusps of a digital revolution where data becomes the linchpin in defining health strategies. Patient records, clinical trials, billing, research, wearable device data all contribute to the burgeoning data reservoirs. Python and Excel, individually known for their data handling abilities, can collectively offer robust solutions for health data management when integrated.

Health Data Extraction using Python

Python's expansive ecosystem of libraries affords it an impressive ability to interact with various forms of data. Excel complements this by offering a popular, universally accepted platform for presenting this data.

To fetch data from electronic health records (EHR), a Python package such as 'FHIR-Python' can be employed.

```python
from fhirclient import client

# Define the FHIR Endpoint
settings = {
    'app_id': 'my_web_app',
    'api_base': 'http://fhir_test_server/api'
}

smart = client.FHIRClient(settings=settings)
search                                      =
MedicationRequest.MedicationRequest.where(struct={})

# Get the Medication Requests on the FHIR server
medications = search.perform_resources(smart.server)
for medication in medications:
    print(medication.as_json())
```

This script interprets medication requests from a FHIR server and prints the output.

Data Cleaning and Transformation

Python's robust data cleaning libraries, such as Pandas, help in rectifying inconsistencies in health data, thereby improving the quality of data analysis.

```python
```

```python
import pandas as pd

# Load the data into a DataFrame
data = pd.read_excel('Health_Data.xlsx')

# Replace missing values with average of column
data.fillna(data.mean(), inplace=True)

# Save cleaned data back to Excel
data.to_excel("Cleaned_Health_Data.xlsx")
```

Python reads data from an Excel file, identifies and replaces the missing values with the mean of each column, and export the cleaned data back to Excel.

Data Analysis and Visualization with Excel

Excel's statistical tools paired with Python's analytical power make for robust data analysis. Excel pivot tables, conditional formatting, charts, and other features help visualize Python-analysed data effectively.

Python, for instance, can process large datasets to extract meaningful statistics, which can then be exported to Excel for visualization and reporting:

```python
# Compute the average age of patients
avg_age = data['Age'].mean()

# Compute the prevalence of a condition, e.g., Diabetes
```

```
condition_prevalence    =    len(data[data['Condition']    ==
'Diabetes']) / len(data)

# Export these statistics to an Excel file

statistics = pd.DataFrame({'Average Age': avg_age, 'Condition
Prevalence': condition_prevalence}, index=[0])

statistics.to_excel("Health_Stats.xlsx")
` ` `
```

"Navigating Health Data Landscapes with Python and Excel:
Enabling Smarter Healthcare Decisions."

Taking on the challenges of health data management with
Python and Excel equips us with a better understanding
of health dynamics and makes way for informed healthcare
decisions. As we sieve through layers of health data and
transform them into practical insights, we tap into the
potential of personalized care, preventive health, and efficient
healthcare delivery. Embracing Python and Excel for health
data management ushers us into a new era of smart healthcare
powered by informed insights.

Operational Analytics

As we delve further into transforming Python and
Excel-enabled capabilities from theoretical promises to
concrete breakthroughs, we arrive at Operational Analytics: a
pivotal realm of the modern business world. As complex as it
sounds, operational analytics entails utilizing data, statistical
algorithms, and Python's machine learning techniques
coupled with Excel's processing power to identify valuable
patterns and insights in operational data. This chapter will
unveil how Python and Excel can be the magic wand that
transforms a deluge of operational data into clear, action-

oriented insights.

Embracing Python and Excel: A New Way to Perceive Operational Data

Operational data is characterized by constant changes, incredible volume, and the complexity of information it comprises. Successful operational analytics is about effective data management, processing, and analysis, and this is what the Python-Excel alliance is conducive to achieving.

Leveraging Python for Data Collection, Processing, and Preparation

Python simplifies data collection and classification from disparate sources - an essential step in operational analytics. For example, using libraries like Scrapy and BeautifulSoup, Python is proficient in data scraping.

```python
import requests
from bs4 import BeautifulSoup

response = requests.get('http://companywebsite.com/')
soup = BeautifulSoup(response.text, 'html.parser')
titles = soup.find_all('title')

# Collecting titles as operational data
titles_list = [title.get_text() for title in titles]
```

This Python code scrapes operational data from a company website, collecting page titles into a list. Preparing and pre-processing data for subsequent steps are simplified by Python's ability for handling, manipulating and cleaning data structures.

```python
# Clean and restructure with Pandas
import pandas as pd

dataframe = pd.DataFrame(titles_list, columns=["Title"])

# Clean up title names
dataframe['Title']        =        dataframe['Title'].str.replace("\n",
"").str.replace("-", "").str.strip()

# Export to Excel
dataframe.to_excel("Clean_Operational_Data.xlsx")
```

In this Python script, Pandas is used to clean and restructure the scraped data, which is then written to an Excel file for further analysis.

Amplifying the Analyses Power with Python and Excel

Excel's wide array of built-in functions and statistical capabilities makes it an adept tool for performing detailed analyses of the operational data. Combining this with Python's ability to process complex data structures and execute high-performing computations results in an environment that supports advanced analytics.

A Python code can be used to analyze operational data, such as identifying trends or detecting anomalies. The analysis results can then be exported to Excel for visualization.

```python
# Analyzing trends using rolling averages
dataframe['Rolling Average'] = dataframe['Operational Metric'].rolling(window=3).mean()

# Export to Excel
dataframe.to_excel("Operational_Analysis.xlsx")
```

This code calculates the rolling average of an operational metric from the data, providing insights into trends.

Visualizing and Reporting Operational Data with Excel

Finally, Excel's rich suite of data visualization tools allows for vibrant, understandable, dynamic dashboards and reports derived from the Python-analyzed operational data.

Reimagining operational analytics through the lens of Python and Excel opens a world where cryptic data transforms into actionable insights, where patterns are discerned amidst apparent randomness, where business operations are seen not just as independent functions but as interconnected workings of an entire system. Marshalling the Python-Excel synergy for operational analytics can lead to smarter decision making, optimized operational efficiencies, and ultimately, a profound impact on the bottom line. The wave of operational analytics, powered by Python and Excel, is here: ride it well and watch your operations thrive.

Customer Relationship Management (CRM)

Serving as the interface between a business and its customers, Customer Relationship Management (CRM) presents a unique challenge that calls for a harmonious fusion of data management and interpersonal communication. As Python and Excel take center stage in this symbiotic ballet of software sophistication, CRM can be transformed from a choreographed routine into a spontaneous dialogue with customers. Let us take a guided tour of the landscape where CRM intersects with the power of Python and the versatility of Excel.

Harmonizing Python and Excel in CRM Symphony

Leveraging Python's data handling strengths and Excel's user-friendly interface can result in a more streamlined, effective, and efficient CRM system. Python's versatile libraries can greatly simplify data retrieval and management, while Excel's powerful features can be harnessed for data visualisation and reporting.

Mining CRM Gold with Python

The first stage consists of gathering CRM information. Lip-plates of data are scattered across different sources - website interactions, emails, call logs, social media, and more. Python libraries like requests and BeautifulSoup can mine these disparate sources to assemble a consolidated dataset.

```python
import requests
from bs4 import BeautifulSoup

# Extract list of customer interactions
url = 'http://crmwebsite.com/interactions'
response = requests.get(url)
soup = BeautifulSoup(response.text, 'html.parser')

# Parse and clean the data
interactions = soup.find_all('interaction')
cleaned_interactions = [interaction.text.strip() for interaction in interactions]
```

This Python script collects interaction data from a CRM website and cleans the data ready for analysis.

Python-Excel Duo for Data Transformation

CRM data needs to be cleaned and transformed into a structured, Excel-friendly format. Here, Python's pandas library shines, enabling us to clean and reshape the data.

```python
import pandas as pd

# Prepare data frame
df              =              pd.DataFrame(cleaned_interactions,
```

```
columns=['Interaction'])

# Export to Excel
df.to_excel('CRM_Interactions.xlsx', index=False)
```

With a bit of Python magic, the raw CRM data is transformed into a structured spreadsheet format.

At this point, we have all our CRM data, clean and structured, sitting splendidly in an Excel sheet. Excel's data visualization features come in handy to create interactive dashboards, giving you a dynamic snapshot of your CRM data.

Unlocking Predictive CRM with Python

Lastly, Python's machine learning libraries can help anticipate customer behaviour and trends. You can train models to forecast sales, predict churn, segment customers, and offer personalized engagement.

Below is an example of a Python code that predicts customer churn based on interaction history.

```python
from sklearn.ensemble import RandomForestClassifier

# Prepare feature matrix and target array
X = df.drop('Churn', axis=1)
y = df['Churn']
```

```
# Fit model
model = RandomForestClassifier()
model.fit(X, y)

# Predict churn
predictions = model.predict(X)
```

The code uses the RandomForestClassifier from scikit-learn, a Python machine learning library, to predict customer churn based on the CRM interaction data.

As we wrap up our exploration of CRM in the Python-Excel matrix, what emerges is not merely an integration of tools but an amalgamation of strengths. With Python and Excel as twin pillars, CRM can evolve from a transactional record-keeping system to a platform for intelligent customer engagement. By harnessing this Python-Excel combination, we can weave a new narrative for CRM that is not just about managing relationships but about nurturing conversations.

CHAPTER 12: BEST PRACTICES FOR EFFICIENT INTEGRATION

Best Practices for Efficient Integration

Journeying into the realm of Python and Excel takes us across landscapes of data management, financial computing, and business modeling. The encounter can be as harmonious as a tea ceremony or as chaotic as a tempest depending on how we orchestrate the integration. In this section, let us uncover the wisdom and practices that can enable efficient integration between Python and Excel, thereby transforming complexity into simplicity, obstacles into stepping stones, and efforts into results.

The Practice of Preparedness: Setting the Stage

Before beginning the process of integration, prepare your environment. Ensure you have the latest versions of Python, Excel, and important Python libraries such as xlwings, openpyxl, and pandas. This diligence in technical setup can smooth your path, preventing unnecessary detours and roadblocks.

The Art of Modularisation: Divide and Conquer

One best practice for efficient Python-Excel integration is modularisation. This involves organising your Python code into separate functions and modules that each perform a specific task. Modularisation helps to keep your codebase clean and organised, which in turn makes it easier to understand, maintain and troubleshoot.

Coherence and Compatibility: Speaking the Same Lingo

Python and Excel, albeit powerful individually, have different lingo - formulas in Excel, modules in Python. Leveraging libraries like xlwings, you can create a bridge that allows Python and Excel to interact seamlessly. Named ranges, cell addresses, formulae translations happen effortlessly with xlwings.

Automation, the Espresso Shot of Efficiency

Efficiency in Python-Excel integration is often synonymous with automation. By automating repetitive tasks in Excel using Python, you save considerable time and decrease the chances of manual errors. Use Python scripts to move data between Excel and databases, to perform complicated calculations, or to create and modify Excel charts, all in a blast.

```python
import xlwings as xw
# Create a new Excel workbook
wb = xw.Book()
```

```
# Reference the active sheet
sht = wb.sheets['Sheet1']
# Write data to the sheet
sht.range('A1').value = [['Data 1', 'Data 2'], [10, 20]]
```

This code snippet creates a new Excel workbook and enters data into it, automating the process of creating and populating a workbook.

Excel Power with Python Precision

Leverage the power of Python for heavy data manipulation and computational algorithms, but leave the presentation, reporting, and quick analysis to Excel. This game of to strengths facilitates the best outcomes.

Python Packaging: Delivering your Solution

Using Python tools to package your solution for easy distribution is paramount. Tools like PyInstaller help to bundle your Python code, modules, and associated resources into standalone executables. These can be run to perform your automated workflows anytime, anywhere with zero dependencies.

Handling Errors Gracefully

Errors are a part of any complex system - a necessary evil. Building robust error-handling into your Python-Excel system can shield users from implementation details, lessen the impact of issues, and provide you with helpful diagnostic information. Python's try-except blocks provide an effective way to achieve this.

```python
try:
    # code that could generate an error
except Exception as e:
    # handle the error
    print(f"An error occurred: {e}")
```

In this Python code, a try-except block is used to catch and handle errors gracefully.

Reflecting on the principles and practices of efficient Python-Excel integration, we see an image of harmony emerging. With Python's computational prowess and Excel's user-friendly interface playing in concert, the cacophonous discord transforms into a symphony of seamless integration. As we learn to direct this concert with best practices, our journey in the Python-Excel realm evolves into an art of molding chaos into order, complexity into simplicity, and efforts into rewarding successes.

Code Documentation

Code documentation refers to the comments and readable text embedded within the script. It serves to explain the lines of code, providing the rationale behind their presence, clarifying complex segments, and defining their responsibilities. It's akin to a map for code, guiding those who dare to venture into this vast territory.

The purpose of code documentation extends beyond serving as a memo. It sets the stage for effective collaboration, accelerates troubleshooting, facilitates smooth updates, and prepares the code for sustainability. Without documentation, the code becomes a cryptic enigma, more challenging than the original problem it sought to solve.

The Anatomy of Well-Documented Code

Good code documentation is concise, relevant, and precisely positioned. It stewards the readers through the code, highlighting the focal variables, functions, modules, and their connections.

At a micro-level, one must describe the variables, functions, inputs, outputs, and logic behind each line. Take a look at an exemplary line of documentation within a Python function:

```python
def calculate_roi(investment, net_profit):
    """
    Calculate the Return on Investment (ROI).

    Parameters:
    investment (float): The initial investment in dollars.
    net_profit (float): The net profit made in dollars.

    Returns (float): ROI expressed as a positive percentage.
    """
    return (net_profit / investment) * 100
```

` ` `

The help doc string provides succinct definitions of both inputs, the output, and the overall function.

At a macro-level, documenting code includes a broad overview, explaining the script's purpose, the role of classes and methods, and the flow between different sections. A summary of the script at the beginning as a multi-line comment or readme file adds an additional layer of clarity.

Best Practices for Code Documentation

Ensure your comments are beneficial and don't state the obvious. Effective documentation does not describe "what" the code does—a competent programmer can deduce this from the syntax—but rather "why" it functions in that particular manner or "how" it achieves its purpose.

Document code as you write, not as an afterthought. Trying to document everything after you've finished coding can lead to forgetfulness and misinterpretations. Coding and documenting should be parallel processes.

Adhere to a chosen style guide for consistency. Whether it's Google Python Style Guide or some other format, a consistent style ensures your documentation is organized and easy to read.

Automate where possible. For example, the Python package Sphinx can auto-generate documentation from your annotations and comments.

In the dance of Excel-Python integration, writing comments

and annotations may feel like a detour from the rhythm. However, effective code documentation serves as an anchor, providing relief to those who must understand, use, or modify the code – including your future self.

Version Control

Imagine a timeline where every modification of your Python Excel integration code left an indelible mark. Each keystroke, each variable change, each newly structured function — all captured, frozen in time. Now imagine being able to traverse this timeline, revisit past versions of your code, and trace lines of modules just like lines of time radiating from an epicenter - that's the essence of version control. As we unlock more doors in the Python-Excel tower, let's board the time machine of version control and learn how it ensures our tower stands tall, no matter the timeline.

Version control, also called source control, manages changes to source code over time. It's like a time machine that allows you to trace the code evolution, track individual elements of adjustments, and even revert to a previous state if needs be. But its scope extends far beyond just a timeline. It serves as a fundamental pillar to collaborative work, a buffer against unexpected bugs, and a catalyzer to swift program updates.

Without version control, you risk trapping yourself in a spaghetti bowl of code, scrambling to remember what was modified when and why. Tasked with a feat of time travel—with a brain that is sadly not equipped to perfectly preserve past states—you won't fare well. Python-Excel integration in such a chaotic environment would amount to building a castle on a quicksand foundation.

Version control systems (VCS)

Two types of version control systems exist – centralized and distributed.

In a centralized system, such as Subversion (SVN), there's a single, central copy of your project on which everyone works. This central copy, or 'repository,' tracks all changes so that you can revisit a previous version of your code anytime. But it has a significant drawback: if the central server fails, you lose access to everything—code, changes, history, etc.

Distributed version control systems (DVCS) like Git solve this single point of failure issue. They clone the entire repository, including its full history, onto your local machine. Even in the face of server failure, a team having access to any of these clones can still recover everything.

Git: The Go-To Solution

Git, due to its blazing speed, robust performance, and stellar support for distributed, non-linear workflows, has become the de facto version control system for countless programmers. It's also a crucial tool in Python-Excel integration projects.

Here's a Python function committed to a Git repository:

```bash
$ git init
Initialized empty Git repository in /.git/
$ echo "def greet(): print('Hello, World!')" > greetings.py
```

```
$ git add greetings.py

$ git commit -m "Initial commit : Add greetings function"

[master (root-commit) 35a31b9] Initial commit : Add
greetings function

1 file changed, 1 insertion(+)

create mode 100644 greetings.py
```
` ` `

The commands above initialize a Git repository, add a function to a Python file, stage the changes, and finally, commit these changes to the repository.

Best Practices: The Wise Ways of Version Control

Each commit in version control should ideally represent a single, coherent change to your code. A clear commit message describing the changes aids future reference.

Ensure you frequently commit your changes. Maintaining small, atomic commits not just simplifies understanding code evolution but also makes troubleshooting easier when things go awry.

Maintain separate 'branches' of your project to work on different features concurrently without affecting the 'master,' or main, line of development. Merging them upon their completion keeps the master repository up-to-date with all the working changes.

Leverage the power of '.gitignore' files to avoid committing unnecessary files (such as those produced during program execution or user-specific settings) into the repository.

Version control, in essence, is the art of time-travelling, minus the paradoxes. It fosters the best of development practices, safeguards your code from potential mishaps, and makes collaboration a breeze. Thus, whether you're crunching data with pandas or crafting visualizations with matplotlib for integration with Excel, navigating with version control by your side equates to sailing with an infallible radar.

In the grand tapestry weaving Python with Excel, version control spins the threads of continuity, turning a tangled skein of code into a timeline that's traceable, sustainable, and tangible. It's the stroke of a sorcerer that does not alter time but merely records it, marking our progress and our regress, our strides and our stumbles. It's as much a crystal ball as a time machine, predicting possible issues by revisiting past bugs. Employing version control is an affirmation of the duality of coding – it's both an art and a science, an act of creation and an embodiment of discipline. It's a journey through times and codes, a journey worth embarking on.

Debugging Techniques

As you explore the intertwining paths of Python and Excel, you may encounter a few stumbling blocks. Here's the good news: getting lost is not a catastrophe. It's a call to disarm the roadblocks on your Python-Excel journey. These roadblocks are often errors lurking in your code, misleading calculations, inaccuracies in data manipulation, or blips in data interpretation. This journey of clarifying your trenches and smoothing your edges commands a new type of sorcery: the art and science of debugging. Welcome aboard this expedition where every cryptic error is a maze, and your investigative cognition is the compass guiding you towards successful Python-Excel integration.

Debugging: The Heart of Programming

Debugging is an integral part of programming. It's the process of identifying, isolating, and fixing errors, or 'bugs,' in your code. Be it a semantic mishap, a logical disorder, or a syntax error, debugging equips you with the necessary torchlight to illuminate these dark corners. The path is often steep, winding through stacks of code, but the rewards are monumental: a clean, efficient, and robust Python-Excel integration.

Entering the Fight: Debugging Python

To wield the sword of debugging efficiently in Python, one must familiarise themselves with the battlefield: error messages. Python throws error messages when it encounters something it can't process. It not only tells you where it faced the hiccup (file name and error line) but also discloses the error type. Knowledge is power, and decoding these messages is the first step towards fixing the faults.

Let's say while integrating Python's pandas library to analyze an Excel dataset, you encountered a `ValueError: cannot convert float NaN to integer`. This message clearly indicates that Python is trying to convert a not-a-number (NaN) value into an integer, which it cannot process.

Python's built-in debugging tool, `pdb`, proves invaluable for navigating through complex code. You can set breakpoints in your scripts, where the program will pause, and let you inspect the variables, step through the code, and extend your understanding of the code's behaviour.

Below is a snippet of a Python script integrated with an Excel range:

```python
import pdb
import pandas as pd
import numpy as np

data = {'A': pd.Series([1, 2, np.nan], index=['row1', 'row2', 'row3'])}
df = pd.DataFrame(data)

pdb.set_trace()

filtered_df = df[df['A'].notnull()]
```

Running this script initiates an interactive debugging session at the line where `pdb.set_trace()` is called. This lets you explore the state of your DataFrame before the filter operation.

Debugging Excel - Meet VBA

Visual Basic for Applications (VBA), Excel's programming language, offers its debugging environment. Tools like stepping through the code (F8), setting breakpoints (F9), and inspecting variable values (hovering over variables/runtime data inspection) are all part of the VBA arsenal.

Excel also has tools to fix formula errors with trace precedents and trace dependents, revealing a map of cells impacting your formula or being impacted by it. The option to display formula values instead of formulas (by pressing `Ctrl + ~`) also simplifies the process of detecting what actual values are being used in your computations.

Embracing Debugging

Debugging also comes with a necessary shift in the mindset. Errors should not be perceived as damning verdicts but as light-posts guiding you where your attention is needed. The bugs are not in your code to embarrass you, but to teach you. They hone your problem-solving skills, polish your programming acumen, and help you refine your approach.

In this debugging journey, patience is your faithful companion. The bugs may be elusive, playing hide-and-seek in loops or conditional blocks; they may be unpredictable, causing irregular software behaviour; or they may be vanishing bugs, disappearing before being isolated for a fix. Patiently untangling the knots and persistently pursuing the solution paths yields not just an error-free code, but also nurtures your growth as an adept Python-Excel integrator.

Debugging diffuses the cloud of confusion shrouding your code, illuminating the Path towards a refined Python-Excel integration. It's indeed an artefact of precision – an art that transforms our code's abstract labyrinth into a precise sketch of sequences and an exacting science that dissects our code into its elemental fragments, offering clarity and control over our creation. On this journey, you're not merely rectifying errors. Instead, you're refining your perspective towards errors, imbibing patience, inculcating an eye for detail, and nurturing a mind that embraces the opportunity of growth nestled within each bug. So, trod along, wield your debugging wand, and blaze a trail of Python-Excel in these code forests!

Unit Testing

In the realm of Python-Excel integration, a robust and error-free code is our prime pursuit. Conquering the bug-demons with debugging is breathtaking, but what if we could prevent the horde from ever touching our sacred code sanctuary? Sounds enchanting, right? Well, it's more than an enchantment. It's the very reality offered by our proactive vanguard: Unit Testing. As heralds of precision and accuracy, let us traverse this riveting vista of unit testing, and infuse our Python-Excel endings with happy, error-free beginnings.

Unit testing is a method of software testing where individual pieces of your code, typically functions or methods, are tested to ensure that they behave as expected. Unit here refers to the smallest testable part of a software - hence the name. Our aim is to attest that each isolated part of the program acts correctly, providing a solid foundation upon which your Python-Excel integration can effortlessly flourish.

Python offers the `unittest` module, patterned after the xUnit framework. This powerful module allows you to create and run test cases, assert outcomes, and report results, therefore forming the cornerstone of your code's integrity.

Let's presume we have an Excel related function that uses Python's `xlwings` library to fetch a range of data. We'll run a unit test to ensure it works as expected.

```python
import unittest
import xlwings as xw
```

```
def excel_to_list(file_path, sheet, range_start, range_end):
    wb = xw.Book(file_path)
    sht = wb.sheets[sheet]
    range_data = sht.range(f'{range_start}:{range_end}').value
    return [item for sublist in range_data for item in sublist]

class TestExcel(unittest.TestCase):

    def test_excel_to_list(self):
        result = excel_to_list('test.xlsx', 'Sheet1', 'A1', 'A3')
        self.assertEqual(result, [1, 2, 3])

if __name__ == '__main__':
    unittest.main()
```

The module `unittest` provides a rich set of tools for constructing and running tests. This unittest checks the function `excel_to_list` to ensure it is converting the excel range data to a flattened list correctly. If our function doesn't behave as anticipated, it's caught dutifully by our unit test.

Excel's VBA also allows unit testing through frameworks like 'VBA-tools/VBA-Unit'. You can write tests for your VBA functions and procedures, and maintain a rigorous check on Excel's functional efficacy.

Unit testing proactively captures errors and improves the robustness of your code. Each test serves as a thread, weaving together a durable safety net catching bugs before they wreak havoc. They also facilitate cleaner code, since writing tests for functions usually forces the use of smaller, more manageable pieces of code.

It is your reliable guard, checking consistently that your software behaves correctly after every modification or addition, reducing bugs in new and existing features. But perhaps its greatest boon is how it instils confidence. You can bravely introduce improvements, assured that your tests will catch any disruption caused.

Your Python-Excel integration benefits immensely from unit testing. Functions of data cleaning, transformation, financial modelling, or even importing Excel data into Python's environment are all critical tasks. Ensuring these operations run flawlessly holds the key to a successful integration. Unit testing shoulders this responsibility, allowing your integration to stand tall amidst the waves of complexity.

Unit testing is the unsung hero of coding, working hard in the shadows. By maintaining meticulous checks on each fragment of your Python-Excel integration, it ensures your final tale is one of precision, accuracy, and excellence. It might seem like an addition to your workload, but in truth, it's a boon bestowed on your code, saving you countless hours spent in error hunting. The essence of unit testing lies in its simplicity - simple tests fostering a complex, well-oiled integration machinery. Embrace this unsung hero and let this vanguard ensure that your every Python-Excel conquest resonates with precision and perfection!

Dependency Management

In software jargon, a "dependency" refers to a

software package, library, or module that your program needs to function correctly. As your Python-Excel application grows, the number of such dependencies scales up. If not adequately managed, these dependencies may result in confounding issues, leading to the infamous "dependency hell". Dependency management is the role of handling these dependencies to ensure smooth application performance, maintaining a balance between diversity in functionality and collecting unnecessary or conflicting modules.

Why is Dependency Management Needed?

The interdependence between software packages is a tale as old as software development itself. When Python meets Excel, their partnership broadens the dependency landscape. Data manipulation utilities like `pandas`, complemented by data parsing libraries like `openpyxl` or `xlwings`, enrich the feature offering enormously. But with multiple dependencies, the risk of version conflicts, outdated modules, and multiple teammates adding redundant libraries escalates, threatening the integrity of the application. Efficient handling and management of these dependencies become an integral part of application development, an answer to application stability and upgradability.

Python's Built-in Virtuoso: pip

Python's native package installer, `pip`, is a versatile dependency management tool. It not only allows you to install and uninstall Python packages but also helps manage them efficiently.

Consider a scenario where we need to use `xlwings` library for our Python-Excel collaborative feat. The command `pip install xlwings` will add the package to our Python environment.

To ensure compatibility across different systems or to resolve conflicted packages, `pip` offers the concept of "requirements files". A requirements file is a list of all dependencies required for your project with their specific versions. To create this file, use `pip freeze > requirements.txt`. This command writes all installed libraries in your environment along with their installed versions in a file named `requirements.txt`.

To replicate the same environment elsewhere, all one needs to do is run `pip install -r requirements.txt` on the new system. As such, `pip` efficiently handles an essential part of Python's dependency management.

Rising Stars: Poetry and Pipenv

While `pip` boasts significant features, the Python community has fostered other tools like `Poetry` and `Pipenv`. These tools combine the functionality of `pip` and `virtualenv` into a single, straightforward tool, helping manage dependencies and virtual environments simultaneously.

Dependency Management Good Practices

With the theoretical understanding in our quiver, let's translate understanding to practice. Here are some best practices for dependency management:

1. **Minimalistic Approach**: Aim to use the least number of dependencies necessary. Each new dependency is a potential entry point for bugs or security vulnerabilities, so consider

whether it's truly necessary.

2. **Updated Libraries**: Consistently update your libraries. This practice equips you with optimal security patches and features.

3. **Use Dependency Management Tools**: Utilise tools like `pip`, `pipenv`, or `poetry` for organising your dependencies.

4. **Document Your Dependencies**: Create a `requirements.txt` or equivalent to note down all dependencies and their versions for easy replication.

5. **Handle Version Conflicts**: Versions of dependencies in your application should be in harmony to prevent conflicts.

Resources and References for Further Learning

One of the most powerful sources of knowledge is the community itself. Q&A websites, forums, and social media groups often provide a plethora of information, catering to questions from beginners and advanced users alike. Websites like Stack Overflow and Reddit are treasure troves of real-world solutions and professional guidance.

Python's Official Documentation

The official Python documentation, reachable at python.org, is a comprehensive guide to the Python language, its standard library, and several other topics. The readability and simplicity of the content presented make the official documentation the first go-to stop for understanding Python concepts, datatypes, libraries, and more.

Data Science Libraries

Libraries like `numpy`, `pandas`, `matplotlib`, `seaborn`, `scikit-learn`, and others have thoroughly documented websites, providing detailed information about their classes, methods, and functions, supplemented by examples. These are fantastic resources when finding your way with data manipulation, visualisation, or machine learning.

Microsoft Excel Documentation

Microsoft's own resources can be handy. The official Microsoft Excel documentation provides essential information related to Excel functions, features, and add-ins. Tips and techniques to handle data analysis in Excel, understanding Excel's computational capabilities, information about Excel VBA, and more are included here.

Python-Excel Libraries

Resources related to Python libraries for Excel interaction, like `openpyxl`, `xlwings`, `xlsxwriter`, and `pandas` can be utilized. These resources cover a wide spectrum of use cases, from reading an Excel file to writing data, applying Excel functions, manipulating data, and building complex Excel applications right within Python!

Python for Finance

Books and resources specifically designed for Python in Finance are very insightful. Yves Hilpisch's 'Python for

Finance' provides excellent content to learn how to apply Python to financial markets. There are also plenty of online resources and finance-specific Python libraries like `numpy-financial` and `pyfolio`.

Online Courses

Online learning platforms like Coursera, Udemy, LinkedIn Learning, and DataCamp offer a wealth of courses on Python, Python for Excel, data analysis, machine learning, and more. These courses often provide a structured learning approach, starting from basics and gradually moving to more advanced concepts.

Blogs and Articles

Blogs and articles in the domain of Python, Excel, and data science are enormously beneficial. Content creators like Medium, Towards Data Science, and KDnuggets regularly publish insightful articles, tutorials, and case studies.

GitHub and Open-Source Projects

GitHub, an extensive repository of open-source projects, is an often undervalued yet potent resource. Studying others' code, contributing to open-source projects, or publishing your project provides a hands-on learning experience. Many libraries also share their source code on GitHub, offering a peek into a library's underlying workings.

Python and Excel Books

Books such as 'Automate the Boring Stuff with Python' by

Al Sweigart, 'Python for Data Analysis' by Wes McKinney, or 'Excel 2019 Bible' by Michael Alexander, provide detailed deep-dives into Python and Excel's world. For a more Excel-oriented Python learning, 'Python for Excel' by Felix Zumstein is an excellent choice.

Podcasts and Webinars

Podcasts and webinars, such as 'Talk Python to Me', 'Python Bytes', or 'Excel TV', combine learning with entertainment, often talking about new packages, innovative solutions, or interviews with experts in the field.

Newsletters and Mailing Lists

Newsletters such as 'Python Weekly', 'Pandas Weekly', or 'Awesome Python Newsletter' can keep you updated about new Python trends, tools, libraries, and best practices.

CHAPTER 13: SECURITY AND COMPLIANCE

Data Encryption and Security

In an age when data is heralded as the new oil, its guardianship is paramount. Throughout our voyage from CELLS-FIEs to financial forecasts, we have voyaged through Python's capabilities, dived into the depths of Excel, and traversed the landscapes of their integration. Yet, as we amass this treasure trove of data-driven insights, it is crucial to remember: all wealth needs protection. In this chapter, we will lay the bedrock of data encryption and security in Python and Excel's realm.

In a world where data volumes continue to escalate at an unprecedented pace, data security and encryption have never been more vital. Data breaches can result in severe financial losses, damage to reputation, and loss of customer trust for businesses. Hence securing data, whether at rest or in transit, is no longer optional but a mandate for every modern organization.

Before we dive into the specific techniques and tools, let's understand the key concepts of data encryption and security.

Encryption refers to the process of translating data into another form, called ciphertext, that cannot be easily understood without access to a decryption key. It is used to protect sensitive information from unauthorized access.

Security is a broader term that involves protecting data from any security breaches, damage, or loss. This includes creating various layers of defense and implementing measures to detect, prevent, or respond to security threats.

Excel provides built-in features to protect data and restrict unauthorized access.

Password Protection: This feature allows you to set a password to open or modify an Excel workbook. It deters unauthorized users from accessing the data or making unintended changes.

Read Only: This feature can make an excel file or a specific worksheet read-only, preventing modifications by unauthorized users.

Protect Cell: This feature allows locking specific cells in a worksheet, preventing modification of crucial data.

Data Encryption in Python

Python offers a slew of libraries to implement security and encryption. One of them is the `cryptography` library.

This library provides various methods for encryption such as symmetric encryption, where the same key is used for encryption and decryption, and asymmetric encryption, where different keys are used for encryption and decryption.

Here is a simple example of symmetric encryption using Fernet, which is part of cryptography.

```python
from cryptography.fernet import Fernet
# Generate a Key for encryption and decryption
key = Fernet.generate_key()
cipher_suite = Fernet(key)
# Given a string 'Python for Excel Advanced'
data = b'Python for Excel Advanced'
cipher_text = cipher_suite.encrypt(data)
print('Encrypted data:')
print(cipher_text)
plain_text = cipher_suite.decrypt(cipher_text)
print('Decrypted data:')
print(plain_text.decode('utf-8'))
```

In this example, we have encrypted a simple data string 'Python for Excel Advanced' and then decrypted it, displaying the original plain text.

Beyond encryption, it is also essential to follow secure code practices. Avoid storing sensitive information directly in the code or documentation, consider obfuscating parts of the code that handle sensitive data, conduct regular security audits and ensure to keep your Python version and libraries up to date.

Alongside data encryption and security, also familiarize yourself with data privacy regulations such as GDPR in the European Union, CCPA in California, and PIPEDA in Canada. These regulations require businesses to protect consumers' personal data strictly, with severe penalties for non-compliance.

As data analysts and programmers, we are the custodians of a treasure trove of data. To fail in our duty to protect it is to invite chaos and disaster. The principles of encryption and security that we have embossed today serve as the fortified walls of this fortress, shielding the prized treasure from prying eyes and persistent invaders. As we continue our Python-Excel journey, remember that this fort we build, layer by layer, will stand as the first bulwark against threats that seek to breach our defenses and pilfer our data.

Compliance Standards

Aligning your Python-Excel prowess with compliance standards is more than merely ensuring we do not run afoul. It is an affirmation that we respect and acknowledge the rights of individuals and organizations over their data. This understanding is the cornerstone upon which we build our credibility and trustworthiness. It is the beacon that guides us as we navigate the sometimes-turbulent waters of data privacy and integrity.

Let's start our discourse by defining the term 'compliance standards.' Compliance standards are guidelines and set principles enlisted by governmental bodies and industry organizations to ensure the security and privacy of data that businesses handle daily. Any organization large or small must adhere to these explicitly designed protocols to avert data breaches, misuse, and ensure data integrity in true essence.

Compliance Standards in Context

Given the nature of our work, it's imperative to understand the critical compliance standards our universe pivots around:

General Data Protection Regulation (GDPR): A vital legal framework that sets stringent guidelines for collecting and processing personal information within the European Union.

California Consumer Privacy Act (CCPA): A state statute designed to enhance the privacy rights and consumer protection for residents of California, across all industries.

Payment Card Industry Data Security Standard (PCI DSS): An information security standard for organizations that require handling branded credit cards from the main card schemes.

Understanding these standards is crucial to our Python-Excel journey. Integrating Python with Excel requires a keen understanding of how to safely handle, store, and manage data according to these widely recognized compliance standards.

Excel, for many, is a familiar working environment for data, and ensuring that it falls within compliance requirements is an absolute necessity.

To make Excel CCPA compliant, for instance, remember that

under CCPA, consumers will be able to ask to see all the data a business has saved on them along with a list of all third parties that the data is shared with. This is where proper Excel data management and setting up the Excel sheet with proper data categories come into play.

Excel already has security features such as protecting workbook with passwords and encryption to make sure data does not get into wrong hands. We learned this in a previous chapter but ensuring that these are used in practice is a key step towards making your Excel data GDPR compliant.

Python is also vastly used in finance, analytics, and AI sectors dealing with an enormous amount of data, personal and confidential. Therefore, it is paramount to follow the above mentioned and other relevant legal frameworks and use Python responsibly.

For instance, storing personal data locally for testing purposes should be anonymized beforehand. Carefully handle cookies and remember to encrypt passwords and important information. Cater to data subject access rights. If an individual asks that their data be removed, it should be.

Python also provides options for logging and keeping track of user actions on the software. Python's immense range of libraries can access and process a plethora of data types over the network, which need to be judiciously used by developers acknowledging the gravity of data privacy in today's digital world.

```python
# Here is a Python csv anonymization example using Faker library
```

```
import csv
from faker import Faker

fake = Faker()

# read the original file and anonymize row by row
with open('original_data.csv', 'r') as file, open('anonymized_data.csv', 'w') as outfile:
    reader = csv.reader(file)
    writer = csv.writer(outfile)
    for row in reader:
        # Assuming personal data is in the first and second column
        row[0], row[1] = fake.name(), fake.email()
        writer.writerow(row)
```

In this example, we're reading the original file and replacing the name and email column with anonymized data. This is a simple but crucial step in making sure that when working with personal data we comply with regulations as GDPR and CCPA.

Code Documentation

Coding practices and their documentation is another area to discuss when we talk about compliance. It is essential to comment on the code for better transparency and understanding for self and others. Regular audits of this documentation and updating with necessary comments are highly recommended.

Auditing and Logging

Keeping track of data and its movements is like shining a spotlight on every dip and rise in a mysterious landscape - a landscape that defines our everyday operations. Auditing and logging, as mundane as it might sound, is this spotlight. By illuminating what would likely be left unseen, it offers us insights that empower us to tread forward with confidence and maintain transparency in our interactions.

Auditing and logging are not as dull as they might sound. It's strategic asset management that does more than just record events. It helps monitor performance anomalies, detect policy violations, analyze trends, and facilitate the detection and investigation of security incidents.

In the context of integrating Python with Excel, both auditing and logging play a notable role. They allow us to responsibly monitor our use of Python scripts within Excel, keeping track of data imports and exports, and even performance optimization techniques.

Monitoring scripts, spotting unusual activities, or even gauging performance - these are things you wouldn't necessarily notice when submersed in the daily grind of tasks. When scrutinized, these variables play a significant role in enhancing efficiency and enhancing end results.

Excel itself comes bundled with a host of auditing features that come in handy. Formula auditing, for instance, allows users to graphically display or trace the relationships between cells and formulas with error checking. The trace precedent and trace dependent tools enable users to identify cells that impact the active cell and cells that depend on it, respectively. Excel also has an inbuilt error checking tool that identifies common errors in formulas.

Additionally, activity logging specifics like viewing, editing, and sharing can be tracked, a feature offered by Microsoft 365. Users can see the detailed activity for individual documents, which can be critical if you share your Excel spreadsheets with others or in an enterprise setting.

Python boasts of a flexible logging system that is easy to use and powerfully customizable. Python's logging library allows developers to log events from applications. Event logs can be very beneficial while debugging issues and understanding application behavior.

Python's logging module provides a professional and flexible method to manage logging, allowing you to log at different levels, including DEBUG, INFO, WARNING, ERROR, and CRITICAL. By logging messages at different levels, you can choose at runtime to ignore less severe messages.

A great example is if you're running an Excel to CSV converter python script that is used by multiple members across different teams:

```python
import logging
logging.basicConfig(filename='app.log', level=logging.INFO,
          format='%(asctime)s    -    %(message)s',
datefmt='%d-%b-%y %H:%M:%S')
```

```python
def csv_from_excel(file):
    try:
        logging.info('Starting to convert excel to csv')
        workbook = xlrd.open_workbook(file)
        all_worksheets = workbook.sheet_names()
        for worksheet_name in all_worksheets:
            logging.info(f'Reading                    worksheet:
{worksheet_name}')
            worksheet                    =
workbook.sheet_by_name(worksheet_name)
            with open('{}.csv'.format(worksheet_name), 'w') as
your_csv_file:
                wr           =           csv.writer(your_csv_file,
quoting=csv.QUOTE_ALL)
                for rownum in range(worksheet.nrows):
                    logging.debug('Writing       row       number
{}'.format(rownum))
                    wr.writerow(worksheet.row_values(rownum))
        logging.info('Conversion successful')
    except Exception as e:
        logging.error('Failed to convert to csv')
        logging.error(str(e))

csv_from_excel('your_excel_file.xlsx')
```
```

In this example, we're attempting to convert an Excel worksheet into a CSV file, and logging each step of the process.
```

Logging and auditing are pillars of regulatory compliance. Compliance standards like GDPR, CCPA require organizations to log and monitor access to sensitive data. Any modification of such data must be recorded with a timestamp, the name of the individual who accessed the data, and the changes they made.

The logging practices dictated by such compliances can vary based on the region, data sensitivity, and breadth of the data handled by the organization. However, it is good to have a strong understand how to audit and logging with Excel and python will powerfully aid in your journey.

Role-based Access Control

In the bustling metropolis of data that our Python and Excel operations form, channeling information access becomes not just essential but a challenge. This is where role-based access control (RBAC) comes to the rescue. As effective traffic conductors, RBAC adds direction, clarity, and control to our everyday data dealings.

Role-based access control, or RBAC as it's commonly acquainted, is the approach via which access rights to certain systems, like Python and Excel operations, are assigned based on the roles of individual users within your organization.

It's imperative to understand that roles should not be confused with individuals; a role represents the set of duties or responsibilities that an individual sports in an organization, and not the individual itself. Thus, different individuals can feature the same roles, making the management of their access rights easier and smoother.

In the realm of integrating Excel with Python, RBAC ensures that the right individuals have the necessary access to the right resources at the right times, and for the right reasons.

Why we need RBAC in Excel-Python Integration

As the integration of Python and Excel grows more complex and widespread, the need to assure that only the right people have access to specific operations is more required than ever. With complex automation, data cleaning, statistical analysis, and financial modeling happening across various spreadsheets, RBAC introduces a safeguard to protect sensitive data.

Consider the scenario where a Python script is integrated with Excel to perform precise financial modelling. Access to this script at the wrong hands could lead to data manipulation, data theft, or even erroneous forecasting. RBAC ensures that only qualified individuals with the right role can access this script, thereby guaranteeing the security of the operation.

RBAC in Action with Python for Excel

To better grasp the idea of RBAC, let's take an instance where a Python script has been generated within an Excel workbook to streamline the process of data cleaning, and this workbook is shared across multiple departments like sales, marketing, and finance. Not everyone in every team will need or understand the various operations performed by the script.

By implementing RBAC, we could ensure the marketing team only has access to execute the script while the finance team, which is filled with individuals cognizant of Python coding, could be given access to both execute and modify the script. The sales team, who might only need to see the results from the data cleaning but not any specifics of the operation, could avoid access to the script entirely.

To put this in effect with Python, we can use the pyfilesystem2 library, which provides objects and functions to work with and manipulate file systems. Here's a brief example to showcase an aspect of this:

```python
from fs.permissions import Permissions

# create limited permissions
limited_permissions = Permissions(u'r--r-----')

# apply permissions to a file
os.chmod('my_python_script.py',
limited_permissions.dump())
```

In this simplistic example, we manipulate the file permissions for the file `my_python_script.py` to allow the owner of the script to read it, while specifically limiting rights for all other users.

Achieving Compliance via RBAC

Accuracy, security, and accountability are some of the major reasons industries are mandated by law to comply with certain regulations. One such critical regulation concerns the access and modification rights for data and information.

Roles ensure specific access levels, hence it is easy to track who accessed what, and when. In addition to filling compliance requirements and preventing unauthorized access to sensitive information, RBAC can also minimize the amount of damage that can originate from the abuse of authorized access.

By maintaining logs of access and changes to the Python and Excel integration, organizations can meet auditing requirements for a variety of compliance standards.

Data Validation and Input Sanitization

Conceived as an integral part of any data handling operation, Data Validation is the process of reviewing the data that we plan to use in our Python for Excel operations to ensure its accuracy and completeness. This is carried out by setting a range of conditions or rules that the data needs to satisfy to be considered valid.

In our Python-Excel integration, especially while interacting with user inputs, proper data validation could mean the difference between accurate, speedy operations and erroneous, sluggish ones.

Key considerations when performing data validation include:

- Checks for potential "outliers" or peculiarities in input datasets.
- Verification of the data framework for expected values or formats.
- Checks for missing or null values.

Python's pandas library offers a variety of functions that support data validation, from simple null check functions like `isnull()`, to more sophisticated functionality contained within the `validate` submodule.

Input Sanitization: The Protector from Intrusions

Simply validating data is not enough when you consider the gamut of Python operations with Excel. Another layer of protection that comes into play is Input Sanitization—it entails getting rid of or modifying data that could lead to processing errors or security vulnerabilities.

In the context of Python-Excel integration, unsanitized inputs could lead to unexpected behaviour during the execution of your Python scripts, or worse, could lead to injection attacks that lead to data breaches.

Input sanitization usually takes place after data validation and includes steps such as:

- Removal of leading/trailing whitespaces.

- Conversion of input characters into a standard format.

- Eliminating or escaping potential code injections.

A simple example of input sanitization in Python could involve the usage of the `strip` function to remove extraneous spaces from a string:

```python
raw_input = " unsanitized input "
```

```
sanitized_input = raw_input.strip()  # removes leading and
trailing spaces
```
` ` `

Data Validation and Input Sanitization Beaming Together

Data validation and input sanitization play harmoniously together. Let's spotlight a finance-focused example to illustrate their partnership. Suppose we have an Excel interface that allows users to input the financial figures which a Python script uses to perform financial forecasting.

However, imagine a scenario where a user unintentionally inputs alphabetic characters in the revenue column. If not validated and sanitized effectively, this could lead to misleading results or even application crashes.

Here's where our duo shines. Once the user inputs the data, our data validation process checks each entry for compliance with the expected format – numerical in this case. If it identifies any non-compliant entry, it could either prompt the user to correct the data or consider the data as NaN (Not a Number).

Next, input sanitization takes over. It helps ensure that even if erroneous data slips through, it doesn't harm other elements of our system or pollute our data pool. In the broad picture of Finance, the repercussions of skipping these two effective measures could be huge.

Closing the Loop – A Touch of Automated Testing

While data validation and input sanitization provide a sense of confidence in our data integrity, it's essential to complement these with effective automated testing methods. This includes a combination of unit tests and integration tests.

Automated testing provides an extra layer of assurance on our data validation and sanitization measures. They let us probe our data validation rules and input sanitization mechanisms, ensuring that they efficiently reject invalid inputs and sanitize harmful ones.

For instance, you could develop a set of unit tests in Python using libraries like unittest or pytest to verify the effectiveness of your data validation and sanitization procedures.

Consider the scenario discussed above. An example of a unit test could be to verify if the validation system correctly handles an alphabetic character input in the revenue column.

To sum up, data validation and input sanitization are like the unsung heroes of data handling in Python for Excel.

The testament to accountability in Python-Excel operations is the staunch guardianship of Data Validation and Input Sanitization. With these two by your side, you form an unstoppable trio that thrives on data integrity and security. As we wrap up this section, bear in mind that the depth of these concepts warrants ongoing exploration.

Ethical Considerations

In the tapestry of Python and Excel integration, understanding the contours of ethical considerations is paramount. As we press on in our discourse, it's necessary to take a moment and dwell on this critical aspect that we often skim too lightly. Ethical considerations form the ingredients of integrity; they seal the credibility and reliability of Python and Excel abilities, guiding us toward responsible practice.

Pivotal to any interaction with data is the utmost respect for its ethical use. Ethical considerations transcend daily coding practices and address deeper facets of human rights, privacy, and confidentiality that bolster in the realm of data.

It's tempting to trudge along the fastest path to data-derived solutions, often neglecting the nuances of ethics. However, the power of Python and Excel bequeaths a fair share of responsibility. Every piece of data contains information about individuals or organizations, and to consider it purely as a resource is a folly.

Python, combined with Excel, can process immense amounts of data at an unprecedented pace. These capabilities underline the importance of pledging to ethical considerations.

Data privacy norms necessitate obtaining explicit consent from individuals concerning the use of their data. This applies to both the collection and processing stages of data. As Python and Excel enthusiasts, we must honour the data subjects' rights and their capacity to withdraw consent at any given time.

Another facet of securing dataance involves data anonymization. It involves obscuring personal identifiers in a data set to protect an individual's privacy. Python libraries like Pandas and Numpy can be employed to perform data anonymization while interacting with Excel datasets.

Data Accuracy and Objectivity

In the quest for obtaining actionable insights from data, it's paramount to persistently validate the accuracy of the data. Providing misleading or deceptive outputs affects data integrity and can lead to the downfall of an entire data analysis operation.

Python and Excel make a formidable ensemble for predominant data operations. Nevertheless, maintaining objectivity while executing tasks such as machine learning algorithms or predictive modeling is crucial. Every stage, from data processing to the interpretation of results, demands prudent objectivity to steer clear of biased outcomes.

Open Source Ethics

Python, being an open-source language, propels a sense of community-oriented ethos. Open source doesn't merely hint at the monetary aspect—it represents a collaborative, transparent approach. It is crucial to respect licenses, attribute credit appropriately, and contribute to the community constructively.

Bias and Discrimination

Algorithmic bias can lead to discriminatory outcomes, and the power of Python in conjunction with Excel can sometimes amplify this. From the initial selection of datasets to the development and testing of models, eliminating bias is a linchpin in ethical coding practice. Equal and fair representation of all groups while designing algorithms can lead to more inclusive products and tools.

Ethics Check: Regular Auditing

Regular ethical audits in any data project can act as a powerful tool in ensuring the deployment of ethical norms constructively. Combining this with proactive training and awareness about ethics fosters an environment that consciously prioritizes ethical considerations.

Those who tread the Python and Excel path must strike their chord with ethical considerations. It's not just about delivering exceptional results but about performing within the ethical ambit that respects data privacy, neutrality, and dignity of individuals associated with the data.

Open-source Vs. Proprietary Tools

Progressing through the distinct layers of Python and Excel integration, it's impossible to ignore the conversation around open-source and proprietary tools. Both carry their unique strengths and shades of weaknesses, hence making the choice between them an essential decision for any professional. Let's delve into this vital juncture and explore the interconnected realms of open-source and proprietary methodologies.

Python stands tall as a shining emblem of open-source software (OSS), embodying the virtues of transparency, collaboration, and public accessibility. When we talk about Python for Excel, multiple OSS tools float to the narrative's surface, including Pandas, NumPy, and xlwings, each equipped with potent functionalities and a wide community of ardent developers.

Open-source tools are a breeding ground for innovation due to their inherent principle of collective intelligence. Anyone can inspect, modify, or distribute the software's source code, sparking a continuum of improvements, adaptations, and advancements that proprietary tools often find hard to match. They offer multiple eyes to catch any bugs swiftly and also provide a platform for learning and skill enhancement.

However, open-source tools might lack the specialised customer support and structured documentation that proprietary tools provide. OSS also leans towards the involvement of the community for security issues, which, though powerful, might not provide the immediacy or assurance some might be seeking.

Proprietary Tools: The Fortresses of Specialisation and Support

Proprietary tools, also known as closed-source software, exist as a stark contrast to the open-door policy of OSS. They are owned by individuals, companies, or entities who control the source code. The usual route to use proprietary tools is to purchase them, although some might offer free, limited versions.

Excel, a proprietary software, is a perfect example within our context. It's well-structured, rich in functionalities, and backed by Microsoft's vast resources and support. Proprietary tools also invest heavily in user-friendliness and dedicated customer support, making them ideal for those who prefer an organised, secure, and comprehensive ecosystem.

However, all these perks come with a price tag, which might be steep in some cases. Additionally, being privy to a few makes proprietary tools less flexible than open-source ones, as they don't allow any modifications or customisations to the source code.

Python and Excel: Where Open-source Meets Proprietary

The Python and Excel integration presents a fascinating amalgamation of open-source and proprietary worlds. Here Python's open-source dynamism combines with Excel's established proprietary environment to create a potent mix of transparency, innovation, structure, and support.

In this setting, your choice between open-source and proprietary tools (or a blend of both) would pivot on factors like the complexity of your project, your budget, your dependency on support, or your willingness to collaborate and innovate.

Open-source Vs Proprietary Tools: Striking the Balance

While open-source tools champion flexibility, collaboration, and innovation, proprietary ones offer robustness, dedicated support, and user-friendliness. The choice between the two should thus hinge on your project's demands, the team's skill set, and your long-term vision.

Remember, neither open-source nor proprietary signifies a sure-shot path to success. It's about exercising discernment, analysing the merits and drawbacks of both, and then aligning them with your aspirations in the Python-Excel universe.

CHAPTER 14: FUTURE TRENDS AND EMERGING TECHNOLOGIES

Machine Learning and AI Trends

As we delve into the exciting realm of future trends and emerging technologies, machine learning and artificial intelligence unmistakably stand at the forefront. These spheres carry transformational power to redefine how we interpret data, make decisions, or enhance efficiency, significantly impacting Python-Excel integration. Join us as we navigate through the mires of these dynamic trends, enabling your journey towards a future-facing outlook.

Machine Learning, a subset of AI, has become an intrinsic part of advanced data analysis. It allows machines to learn from previous data, identify patterns, and make data-informed predictions. Python, with its powerful ML libraries like TensorFlow and SciKit-Learn, has been a widely recognised tool in executing ML algorithms.

Within the Python-Excel ecosystem, ML can automate your Excel worksheets to learn from your data and predict outcomes. It eliminates manual predictive modelling while also enhancing prediction accuracy, thereby elevating Excel's capabilities significantly. Imagine creating a sales forecast in Excel, but with an ML model automating the entire process, improving accuracy, and saving time - that's Python and ML taking Excel a notch higher.

The AI Revolution

AI is undeniably transforming how we interact with data. Techniques like Natural Language Processing (NLP) or automation have already begun reshaping various areas, including data analysis, report generation, or customer service.

With Python's AI capabilities combined with Excel's ubiquity and ease of use, the possibilities for disruption are immense. For example, Python's NLP libraries can help in sentiment analysis, while Excel can serve as an accessible interface for the results. This fusion can aid in gaining valuable customer insights, enhancing product development, and improving business strategy.

Adaptive Intelligence in Excel

Envisage feeding your monthly sales data into Excel and having the software automatically lay out future trends. This scenario is now becoming a reality with Adaptive Intelligence in Excel. Excel is already leveraging AI in functions like "Ideas," which applies machine learning to recognise patterns and suggest data illustrations. Python's ML and AI libraries take this a step further and offer precise control over the AI implementation.

Python and AI: Creating Dynamic Dashboards

Creating dynamic, interactive dashboards is where Python's AI capabilities truly shine in conjunction with Excel. One such example is creating an ML model in Python to predict sales trends and then dynamically visualising those predictions in Excel using real-time updates. This blend of advanced prediction and real-time visualisation can form an essential part of data-driven decision making, notably in finance or sales management.

Machine Learning and AI in Financial Analysis

Consider the role of ML and AI in financial analysis—one of the most crucial application areas in the Python-Excel ecosystem. ML models can help in predicting stock prices, credit scoring, risk assessment, or fraud detection while Python and Excel can work together to organise, analyse, and visualise the findings in an accessible and user-friendly manner.

Cloud-based Excel Solutions

Today, we stand at the cusp of a dynamic shift in data processing and storage – a transition from localised hardware to virtual, cloud-based platforms. In this chapter, we chart the potential and promise of this revolution as we explore how Python and Excel are embracing this cloud-based future.

Microsoft Excel's integration with the cloud-based platform - Office 365, has brought an unprecedented wave of flexibility and collaboration in the way we handle spreadsheets. Data can be accessed, analysed, shared and updated in real-time from any device, anywhere, reducing dependency on physical hardware and increasing productivity.

Cloud-based Excel offers features like co-authoring, allowing multiple members to work on the same Excel workbook simultaneously. With real-time syncing, updates made by one user reflect instantly for all others, ensuring everyone has the latest version of the sheet. Team members can also communicate through comments, making remote collaboration seamless.

Python's adaptability and Excel's cloud interface form an impressive partnership. Python scripts that interact with cloud-based Excel worksheets can process data in real-time, enabling dynamic data analyses and visualisations. Also, cloud storage eliminates the need for physical computing resources, making it possible to handle large datasets within Excel, aided by Python's processing capabilities.

The integration of the robust Python language and cloud-based Excel solutions also unlocks access to enormous computing power. Complex analyses and calculations that once strained your local computing capacity can now be performed remotely on powerful cloud-based servers. This computing capacity is especially beneficial when running Python's Machine Learning algorithms on large Excel datasets, delivering faster results and aiding in real-time decision-making.

Moving data to the cloud inevitably presents considerations around data security and compliance. While the cloud poses its own set of challenges, Python's libraries for encryption and secure coding practices can help protect your Excel data. Also, cloud providers often adhere to global security standards, offering features such as data encryption, multi-factor authentication, and access controls, ensuring high-level security for your Excel files.

Cloud-based Excel solutions, complemented by Python's powerful libraries, can dramatically transform data analytics, ushering in an era of improved collaboration and data-driven decision-making. The next frontier of analysis is likely to feature geographically dispersed teams working on shared datasets, highlighting trends and making decisions in real-time.

Consider a sales team analysing customer data stored in a cloud-based Excel sheet, using a Python script to identify patterns in customer behaviour, predict future trends, and display the results in a live dashboard shared across the team. This level of collaboration opens the doors to more informed and timely decisions, increasing efficiency and effectiveness.

The integration of Python with Cloud-based Excel holds promise for a future where bottlenecks in computational capacity, file sharing, and real-time collaboration become artifacts of the past. Leveraging the power of cloud in conjunction with Python and Excel is more than just staying on-trend; it is adapting to the future of data handling and unlocking possibilities we are only starting to imagine.

Decentralized Networks and Blockchain

Our constantly evolving technological landscape is advancing like never before. With Python and Excel's remarkable capabilities in managing and analyzing data, we now delve into a realm that is often elusive yet holds immense potential: The sphere of Decentralized Networks and

Blockchain.

At the core of Blockchain technology is the concept of decentralization, a form of distributed system where operations are not directed from a single, centralized point. Instead, authority and function are spread across a network, fundamentally improving transparency, reducing points of failure, and negating the need for intermediaries.

Python, with its simplicity and robustness has been one of the leading languages in the development of blockchain technologies. Whether you are building a blockchain from scratch or interacting with an established one, Python provides the necessary tools for you.

For Excel users, the drive towards incorporating blockchain comes from the need for a respected, immutable ledgers. By applying blockchain to Excel operations, one can create a fully auditable and tamper-resistant log that grows more secure with each record.

Python's simplicity, versatility, and capability for advanced calculations make it ideal for blockchain programming. Building a blockchain network from scratch involves creating data blocks and linking them securely, a task Python performs with ease, thanks to libraries like hashlib, datetime, and json.

Python's vast collection of libraries facilitate various key blockchain functionalities- from connecting nodes in the network to performing the complex mathematics required for 'mining' or validating transactions.

Moreover, Python is commonly used for developing smart contracts- self-executing contracts with the terms directly written into code. These contracts live on the blockchain and are triggered and executed by specific events or conditions.

In the world of Excel, the application of blockchain opens new doors for secure data management and auditability. Each addition or change made in an Excel sheet can be represented as a block in the blockchain, and as new blocks are added, old ones become almost impossible to tamper with due to the nature of cryptographic linkage.

For instance, Excel could be used to monitor company supply chains by using the functionalities of a blockchain. From the manufacturer to the delivery service, each step could be recorded, creating a permanent history of a product's journey.

When Python, Excel, and Blockchain come together, the possibilities expand exponentially. We potentially have the capability to create smart contracts within Excel, powered by Python. Or enabling Python scripts that interact with blockchain data within Excel, processing and analysing it as necessary.

This combination could facilitate complex systems for data validation. Let's consider an Excel workbook shared by multiple stakeholders, each making changes or additions to the contents. A Python script could be used to push these changes to the blockchain, providing absolute transparency and data integrity.

The advent of blockchain and decentralized networks propels Python and Excel into a new dimension with extraordinary potential. We are glimpsing into a future where Excel can boast of the unprecedented security and transparency that decentralized systems offer and Python, with its simplicity and power, becomes the instrument in navigating this complex realm.

Internet of Things (IoT)

Living in a digital era, we are more connected than ever through an intricate web of devices collectively known as the Internet of Things (IoT). As Python and Excel champions, we seize this opportunity to delve into the fascinating meld where computer science meets physical world. Brace yourself as we start to decrypt the traverse where Python and Excel intersect with IoT, enriching our capabilities of data analysis, device automation, and interconnectivity.

IoT stands for Internet of Things, representing billions of physical devices around the world connected to the internet, all collecting and sharing data. This phenomenal interconnection offers a wealth of data, promising to improve and automate processes in industrial and consumer applications.

From monitoring environmental conditions like temperature and moisture, health tracking through wearables, to automating home devices, IoT is transforming every aspect of our lives. With Python and Excel coming into the mix, we can unlock new potentials, beneficial both to businesses and our everyday lives.

Python, renowned for its efficiency and simplicity, is an ideal language for IoT applications. Whether it's a small device like a Raspberry Pi or a complex industrial system, Python has the adaptability to fit these varying needs.

Python's prowess lies in its ability to handle and process real-time data. With IoT devices emitting colossal amounts of data, Python's data analysis libraries (like Pandas and NumPy) facilitate efficient data analysis. Furthermore, libraries like MQTT provide a lightweight method of messaging protocol, essential for many IoT applications.

Also, Python's multifaceted library support, like GPIO for interacting with hardware pins and Flask for web server development, makes creating and managing IoT devices more accessible. Thus, making Python a popular choice for IoT.

Excel's Role in the IoT Ecosystem

Excel, the long-standing king of spreadsheets, also plays a crucial role in the IoT ecosystem. All the data from various IoT devices need to be laid out, analysed, and visualised effectively. Excel continues to remain a powerful tool for this task.

Excel offers extensive data analysis functionalities and robust data visualization capabilities, enabling users to transform raw IoT data into actionable insights. With the power of Excel, users can discern patterns, trends and anomalies from their IoT data, thereby optimizing and automating processes.

Python, Excel, and IoT: A Powerful Alliance

When the simplicity and versatility of Python, the data crunching power of Excel, and the omnipresence of IoT come together, we witness an extraordinary symbiosis. Together, they form a powerhouse for managing IoT data.

For instance, a Python script could be used to collect data

from various IoT devices, perform initial cleaning and analysis before pushing this data to an Excel sheet. In Excel, a user can then analyse this data further, leveraging Excel's deep suite of analytical tools.

This amalgamation creates exciting possibilities such as smart homes or businesses, where Python scripts embedded in Excel can monitor and control IoT devices. It could be as simple as a Python script in Excel, tracking energy usage in your home, or as complex as managing an entire industrial IoT network.

Moreover, the integration also allows interoperability between devices, which is a foundational requirement in IoT. From Python, we can use protocols such as MQTT to enable communication between devices and from Excel, we can present, analyse, and make data-driven decisions.

The combination of Python, Excel, and IoT has started to shape a future where data from every corner of our world can be captured, analysed and used for smarter decisions and automation. As the IoT network of interconnected devices continue to grow exponentially, the potential of how we can interact and influence our physical world through Python and Excel is also boundless.

Big Data and Data Lakes

As the digital landscape of our world continually expands, we're rapidly moving towards an era where data is the new gold. With petabytes of data being generated every minute, the concepts of big data and data lakes have come to the forefront. This section seeks to untangle the intimate interplay between Python, Excel, and these sprawling data ecosystems while fostering an understanding of their collective impact on business analytics and decision-making.

Big data refers to colossal datasets that regular data processing software cannot handle. These gigantic pools of data promise a wealth of valuable insights that can drive strategic business decisions. From customer behaviour patterns to predictive analyses, big data holds immense potential for those who can harness it effectively.

Here's where Python and Excel come in. Python, with its vast array of machine learning and data analytics libraries like Pandas, Scikit-learn, and TensorFlow, allows us to tackle these vast volumes of data effectively. It provides efficient algorithms to manage, analyze, and visualize big data, making it a popular choice among data scientists and analysts.

Excel, on the other hand, known for its robust UI and intricate data analysis features, provides an ideal platform for the exploration and reporting of these insights crafted by Python. With PowerPivot and Power Query, Excel can load and manipulate large datasets, making it a versatile tool for dealing with big data.

Imagine having a massive reservoir storing a multitude of raw data from various sources, right at your frontend. This is what data lakes offer. They store raw, unstructured data in its original format, meaning you can keep any data, from anywhere, without having it organized first.

Python's superior handling of structured and unstructured data shines in this context. Python allows data engineers to pull data from varying sources, manipulate it, and load it into the data lake. Moreover, Python's excellent libraries like PySpark (for data processing) and SQLAlchemy (for managing

SQL databases), makes processing and analyzing data from the data lakes more efficient.

Simultaneously, Excel's Power Query can tap into data lakes, transforming, cleaning, and shaping data before analysis. Excel's intuitive UI and visualization capabilities make it a preferred tool for many analysts when handling data lake outputs.

In the vastness of big data and the depth of data lakes, Python and Excel find an uncharted playground. Python scripts are capable of mining massive volumes of data, sifting through it, identifying patterns, and extracting valuable insights. Meanwhile, Excel, with its Power Pivot and Power Query functionalities, provides an intuitive and user-friendly interface to investigate and visualize these data-driven insights.

For instance, a Python script may be used to analyze data from a data lake, process it, and run machine learning algorithms to identify patterns. The transformed data could then be exported to an Excel file where its visualization capabilities would come in handy for reporting and decision-making.

The technologies play into each other's strengths perfectly - Python's superior data processing with Excel's user-friendly interface and deep analytical tools, when dealing with the vast data plains of big data and data lakes, creates an efficient, fluid, and powerful workflow.

Furthermore, this dynamic quartet, Python, Excel, big data, and data lakes, make advanced analytics accessible to organizations of all sizes. They create a paradigm where businesses can harness vast datasets' true power, driving strategic decisions, optimizing processes, and forecasting future trends.

The common thread that binds big data, data lakes, Python, and Excel is the endless quest for improved business intelligence and advanced analytics. As we become increasingly data-driven, these technologies have become the guiding light to a future where any data, regardless of size or structure, can be wielded effectively.

The surge in big data has fundamentally revolutionized data lakes' role, and mastering these coalesces with skills in Python and Excel could be an unprecedented advantage. As we navigate further through this data deluge, our ability to leverage these technologies will play a crucial role in shaping a data-driven world wherein we drive strategic decisions, optimize business processes, forecast trends, and achieve peak business performance.

Real-time Analytics and Streaming Data

In a world characterized by rapid digital transformation, the ability to analyze data and extract insight as it arrives – in real-time – is a powerful competitive edge. Real-time analytics refers to the process of delivering insights instantaneously, allowing for decision-making based on real-time data.

Python, with its wide array of dedicated libraries like scikit-learn, TensorFlow, and Keras, proves its mettle in real-time analytics. Be it running a complex deep learning model or functioning as the backend for a real-time dashboard, Python becomes an invaluable tool for data scientists.

On the other side, Excel is tough to beat when it comes to simplicity and familiarity. More recently, Microsoft Power BI, an Excel evolution, has made real-time analytics available to the masses. Combining the analytical power of Excel with real-time capabilities has paved the way for dynamic dashboards that update as the data flows.

Streaming Data: The Lifeline of the Digital Era

Data streaming is the process of sending data records continuously rather than in batch processing. It's a flow of data that reflects events happening in real-time. Data streams may include a variety of data such as log files, real-time market feeds, social media data, and online gaming.

Python, once again, stands out in handling streaming data due to its efficient handling of continuous data flows. Libraries like Kafka-Python and PySpark Streaming allow for building real-time streaming applications, opening up a world of possibilities.

At the same time, Excel offers Power Query, an incredibly powerful data-gathering tool that can talk to many data sources and is capable of handling streaming data. It can interface with various APIs and also interact with real-time data platforms such as Apache Kafka.

Python, Excel, and Real-time Analytics and Streaming Data: A Powerful Trifecta

The ever-evolving capabilities of Python beautifully align with the needs imposed by real-time analytics and streaming data. Python's wide range of machine learning and AI libraries, coupled with its easy-to-use syntax and high speed, make it apt for handling real-time data analysis.

Epitomizing this trend, Python-focused platforms like Streamlit have begun to gain momentum. These help data scientists and Machine Learning (ML) engineers swiftly create apps to visualize insights from ML models.

On the other hand, Excel has evolved to cater to the need to visualize and present the insights derived in real-time beautifully. Leveraging Power BI – a suite of business analytics tools by Microsoft – users can run real-time analytics, produce robust insights, and create stunning reports, interactive charts, and dashboards that update in real-time.

Together, Python and Excel form a potent combination in managing real-time analytics and streaming data. Python efficiently analyzes streaming data as it flows in and derives insights. These insights are then brought to Excel, which acts as an ensemble stage where they come alive through visual presentations, informing strategic, real-time decisions.

Real-time analytics and streaming data have marked a technology turning point. It allows businesses to respond as fast as they receive data. In managing this instant data, Python's efficiency and Excel's interface has proven invaluable, revolutionizing how organizations perceive and handle live data.

Bridging the Real-time Gap: Python, Excel and the New Data Frontier

As the pace of data accelerates and the demand for immediate response soars, the dynamism of real-time analytics and streaming data can no longer be ignored or misunderstood. With Python and Excel, the potent duo for handling these, we stand on the threshold of a revolution that recognizes the 'nowness' of data.

Mastering real-time analytics and streaming data with Python and Excel will not just make you ready for the future; it makes you ready for the now. With this exploration of the transformative world of real-time analytics and streaming data, we paint a horizon where one can make actionable decisions as trends happen, not after they have occurred.

Augmented and Virtual Reality in Data Visualization

Lend me your imagination for a moment. Picture a world where data is not just analysed but experienced, a virtual realm where complex data structures are not just visually translated but virtually interacted with. Welcome to the exciting and immersive landscape of augmented and virtual reality interfacing with data visualization. Journey with me as we explore how Python and Excel serve as architects of this cyberscape, transforming the traditional terrain of data visualization.

Augmented Reality (AR) is a technology that overlays digital information on real-world elements. If we consider data visualization - the representation of data in a pictorial or graphical format, A.R. takes this a step further. It offers an interactive experience of a real-world environment, supplemented by computer-generated perceptual information.

Python steps into this fore with its libraries, like Vuforia, ARToolKit, which offer a veritable toolset for creating augmented reality applications.

Excel, while not traditionally incorporated into augmented reality, paves the way for A.R. experiences through data feeds. Data prepared and organized in Excel can be served to the augmented reality applications for an augmented data experience.

A Dive into Another Dimension: Virtual Reality (V.R.) in Data Visualisation

Virtual Reality (VR), a simulated experience that can be similar to or completely different from the real world, offers a completely immersive method for visualising data. Imagine being able to step 'inside' your data, walking through your data points, and having a spatial and visual understanding of complex multi-dimensional datasets.

Python shows its versatility here as well. Libraries such as Pyglet and Panda3D cater specifically to VR and 3D programming. Pygame, a set of Python modules designed for game creation, can also be harnessed for creating engaging VR data visualizations.

Python, Excel, and A.R./V.R.: Trailblazing the Future of Data Visualisation

Python has become a popular choice in the VR and AR world thanks to its simplicity and the availability of advanced libraries to create engaging VR and AR applications. Furthermore, data organized and processed in Excel forms the backbone of these applications, contributing towards real-time, immersive experiences.

An intriguing example of Python's application in AR is constructing 3D scatter plots using the popular data manipulation library pandas and visualization library matplotlib. Once integrated into an AR application, one could theoretically 'step into' their scatter plot, visually investigating and manipulating their data in previously unimaginable ways.

Excel, when paired with Python, can feed the VR and AR models with real-time data, ensuring that the virtual environments they operate in are always up-to-date and relevant.

In the leap from desktops to AR and VR environments, data visualisations transition from just being helpful analytical tools to full-fledged experiential stories that allow users to interact with and draw insights from data in an entirely novel way. For instance, financial analysts could use VR to physically navigate through complex financial models, observing the real-time impacts of different market conditions.

Navigating the Metaverse: Python, Excel and the New Frontier

As we wrap up this exciting exploration of the integration of augmented and virtual reality into data visualization with Python and Excel, we sense a palpable shift in the storytelling of data. The promise of AR and VR is enormous. Instead of viewing static graphs and charts, analysts can immerse themselves into the data, obtaining a spatial understanding of the complex systems at play. We are standing at the threshold of a brave new world, where data interaction veers towards the utterly interactive, intuitive, and immersive.

Thought of using Python and Excel might have been a herculean task in the past, but with initiatives like AR and VR, these tools take on a charisma of their own.

As we continue this journey through the latest trends and techniques shaping the world of Python, Excel, and data handling, remember that we stand at the forefront of an expedition into territories both thrilling and new. The next frontier awaits our exploration, offering challenges and opportunities that promise to shake up our understanding of data interaction. Are you ready for the ride? Join us in the next section as we take you into the captivating universe of big data and data lakes.

Recap of Key Concepts and Takeaways

As we pause in our journey across the rich landscape of Python and Excel's integration, it's an opportune moment to reflect on the ground we've covered, the concepts we've grasped, and the insights we've unearthed. This is the springboard moment, the harbour where knowledge gathered fuels us forward into novel explorations and deeper understanding. This reflective process can help consolidate the gleaned knowledge, making it an empowering exercise.

The journey started with an introduction into the vibrant world of Python and Excel integration, where we saw how the seemingly disparate worlds of a scripting language like Python and a spreadsheet software like Excel harmoniously intertwine. The benefits and advantages of Python over Excel, the power of Excel and how to navigate the Excel-Python interface were all key highlights of our initiation that also included practical usage scenarios.

We delved into Python programming essentials for Excel users and became acquainted with Python's IDEs, its standard library, data structures and importantly, the comparison with Excel's VBA. Transiting into data manipulation and cleaning, we explored how Python and Excel can work together to transform data, perform advanced filtering and even batch processing.

Our exploration of Excel functions and Macros led us to automate repetitive tasks, and work with complex data types and Python classes. Here, we understood the merging of Excel's front-end capabilities with Python's code to develop robust financial models and forecasting, using regression analysis and even Monte Carlo simulations.

The mighty world of Python's Machine Learning capabilities gave a us a taste of predictive modelling, classification algorithms, and anomaly detection all integrated with Excel. This was aptly supported with a walkthrough on creating visually appealing and insightful reports and dashboards.

Our expedition into the realm of performance optimisation had us handling large datasets and parallel processing. Web scraping and API integration was the next frontier we successfully navigated, scraping dynamic websites and working with OAuth and token-based authentication.

Donning the creative hats, we built custom Python tools for Excel, introduced user authentication and authorisation and focused on user interface design principles. Practical applications struck a chord with everyone when we dissected case studies throwing light on how Python and Excel integration could be used in financial data analysis, dynamic reporting, and inventory management, among many other applications.

As we moved towards the end, we navigated the need for code documentation, debugging techniques and resources for further learning in light of best practices for Python and Excel integration. Security and compliance were not left behind as we discussed data encryption, auditing and logging as well as the ethical considerations in the open-source vs proprietary tools debate.

The wave of future trends in emerging technologies led us towards exploring machine learning and AI trends, cloud-based Excel solutions, and decentralised networks or blockchain. The opportunity of leveraging augmented and virtual reality in data visualisation opened a new exciting pathway into the future of Python and Excel.

CHAPTER 15:
CONCLUSION AND
FINAL THOUGHTS

*A Condensed Universe: Python,
Excel and the Continual
Quest for Knowledge*

As we look back, the enormous wealth of knowledge we have gained in the realm of Python and Excel integration shines bright. We have sailed past simple concepts and dived deep into the nitty-gritty of advanced techniques, emerging enriched, enabled and empowered.

Yet, the journey doesn't end here. Like every venture, our voyage has unveiled more paths than it has traversed. There are mysteries still to be solved, secrets still to be unlocked, and tasks still to be accomplished in this vast universe of Python and Excel. So, endure, my companions of knowledge, for the pursuit of wisdom is ceaseless and the harvest fulfilling. Our journey of discovery continues, building upon the sturdy foundation we've laid throughout this book. As our sails catch the winds of progress, we journey forth for more uncharted territories. Let's stride ahead, ready to conquer the insatiable thirst of enquiry!

Final Thoughts and Future Directions

Python and Excel have made an impactful pairing in the world of data analysis and business intelligence. The blend of Python's mettle in robust computation, machine learning, and data manipulation with Excel's superiority in spreadsheet handling, user-friendly interfaces and widespread business use, gives us a powerhouse of capabilities. Yet, as appealing as their synergy is, we are merely at the outset of a boundless journey, for numerous pathways beckon us forward.

With burgeoning developments in artificial intelligence and data science, we anticipate Python's role in Excel to expand exponentially. As data continues to play an increasingly pivotal role in decision-making, businesses will seek more robust, accurate, and flexible tools within their existing frameworks. Python's potential in such scenarios is immense. Whether it's developing more sophisticated forecasting models, applying machine learning techniques for predictive analysis, or crafting intricate algorithms for optimization, Python's versatility can enhance Excel's capacities multifold.

Compatibility is a pressing issue in today's interconnected digital world. Excel's VBA built for Windows struggles to keep up with cross-platform demands. Python, being platform-agnostic, offers a valuable solution. We foresee a trend wherein businesses would transition into Python scripts for their Excel-based automation needs. This ensures interoperability across diverse platforms, giving businesses the flexibility they need.

The democratization of coding points towards a future where the divide between users and developers will blur even more. In such a landscape, the need for building custom Python tools for Excel would rise. Whether it's custom ribbons, user interface designs, or add-ins, Python can offer a host of possibilities for customization in Excel.

Python's prowess in data scraping and API integration indicates a future where real-time Excel dashboards, directly linked to data sources, become the norm. In an age where real-time and well-informed decisions are critical, this integration could revolutionize how we perceive reporting.

Our efforts towards achieving efficiency and improving performance in Excel using Python reveal a promising future. Larger datasets, faster computations, and sophisticated caching techniques will speed up data cleaning, manipulation, and analysis in Excel, making it more suitable for Big Data scenarios.

Security is, and will continue to be, a prominent focus area. As data usage increases, so will the need for secure data handling practices. Python in Excel can offer novel solutions like advanced encryption, more stringent role-based access controls, and improved auditing.

This look into the future is inspiring, but it requirements commitment from us. It demands that we continue learning, exploring, and innovating. We must continuously adapt to emerging trends, harness the power of new developments, and diligently implement what we've learned.

Looking into the future retrospectively, we see an enthralling odyssey of discovery. As we move forward, we will continue to mine the extensive potential of Python in Excel. More than the tools, syntax, or features, it's the principle of continuous learning and improvement that remains intrinsic in us.

Remember, we are navigating uncharted territory. We have been explorers, and as true explorers, we know our exploration doesn't cease. With every question answered, new questions surface; for each problem resolved, other uncertainties arise. This is the perpetual cycle of learning, a never-ending journey imbued with ceaseless curiosity. Unbound and undeterred, we march ahead, for the world of Python and Excel awaits us. To more questions, more solutions, more knowledge, and more power - let's continue striving!

Opportunities and Challenges

The realm of Python and Excel integration opens up a mesmerizing landscape of possibilities, filled with bubbling springs of opportunities and towering peaks of challenges. As competent navigators in this journey, we find ourselves at a unique juncture, where we evaluate our journey thus far and envision our forward path.

As we have embarked on this momentous journey leveraging Python in tandem with Excel, we cannot overlook the myriad of opportunities that lay before us. These opportunities are born from the confluence of the two tools, bringing together the best of both worlds, thereby promising exponential productivity gains and a new perspective on dealing with data.

At the forefront of these opportunities lies the potential to automate repetitive tasks. Python's ability to handle and manipulate vast amounts of data with ease can complement Excel's user-friendly data presentation. Businesses handle innumerable complex and monotonous tasks daily. By integrating Python with Excel, we stand on the threshold of revolutionizing and simplifying these workflows.

The ability to perform complex data analysis and create advanced algorithms is another significant opportunity. Python, by its inherent nature, allows for more complex statistical analyses than those available in Excel. Integrating the two allows for sophisticated data handling capabilities on readily available and familiar platforms—unlocking potential unheard of until very recently.

With the explosive growth of machine learning, bringing these capabilities into Excel could be a game-changer. By using Python's extensive ecosystems of libraries like TensorFlow or ScikitLearn, machine learning can be brought directly to your spreadsheets. From predictive analysis to classification and regression models, we have the opportunity to harness this rapidly advancing field in our favourite data software.

Python also offers extensive tools and libraries for data scraping and web automation, which, when incorporated into Excel, provide powerful features for collecting data in real-time. This would transform Excel into a dynamic data analysis tool where the data is always up-to-date.

However, every silver lining comes with a cloud, and the merger of Python and Excel isn't bereft of challenges. Notwithstanding the alluring opportunities, it's inherently crucial that we navigate through these challenges to ensure the full potential of this integration endeavor.

The learning curve serves as the most significant challenge. Despite Python's relatively straightforward syntax, it still requires a fundamental understanding of programming. Existing Excel users who are familiar with point-and-click interfaces may find this initially intimidating. It will be essential to create effective and accessible training materials that can guide users through this transition.

Another challenge is the wide array of Python versions and packages. Ensuring compatibility can soon turn into a complex task. Python scripts developed with a specific version or set of packages may not work as intended in a different setup. Care must be taken to ensure that appropriate versioning and package management practices are in place.

From a security perspective, running Python scripts in Excel workbooks can pose potential threats. Indeed, Python has far-reaching abilities and can potentially perform actions that go beyond the workbook, including filesystem operations, network communication, and much more. Protecting against malicious use is a challenge that needs addressing.

The fact remains that Python was not initially designed for integration with Excel. There might be areas where the integration is not as smooth or efficient as one might wish. Overcoming these design limitations will demand innovative thinking and diligent programming.

The integration of Python with Excel presents us with a promising but challenging landscape. The terrain undulates with the highs of opportunities and lows of challenges, presenting a paradox of sorts. A paradox that leads us to believe in the immense potential that lies ahead, yet demands a thorough comprehension of the trouble spots.

The Ecosystem of Python and Excel Tools

On the frontier of Python and Excel integration, lies an intricate ecosystem of tools and technologies that drive the seamless fusion between these two powerful platforms.

This carefully curated assembly of Python modules, add-ins, libraries, and Excel's distinguished features is managed in an omnipresent environment of harmony and synergy.

This rich ecosystem begins with Python itself, a versatile and robust programming language characterized by its simple yet effective design. The power of Python lies in its extensive and diverse assortment of libraries and packages, which function as agents for varied tasks, be it data manipulation, visualization, statistical analysis, machine learning, and much more.

At the core of the Python-Excel integration stands the colossal bridge that binds Python and Excel together - xlwings. An open-source Python library, xlwings allows for automation and interactive handling of Excel files. It equips the developer with capabilities to read, write, and manipulate data, while also enabling the creation of user-defined functions (UDFs). With xlwings operating under the hood, Python scripts can be triggered directly from Excel, fusing the Pythonic power with Excel's widespread familiarity in a symbiotic embrace.

On the same note, another tool worth mentioning is PyXLL. Tailored specifically to cater for financial analysts and quantitative researchers, PyXLL allows Python functions to be directly used as Excel functions, while also supporting asynchronous tasks and macros. This enables users to harness Python's computational strength directly within their Excel workbooks.

For scenarios demanding extensive data cleaning and manipulation, Python's pandas library comes to the rescue. This powerful data manipulation tool provides crucial functionalities like reading and writing Excel files, handling missing data, merging datasets, and much more.

To further enrich our data processing capabilities, we rely on libraries like NumPy and SciPy. NumPy introduces high-dimensional array objects that facilitate efficient multi-dimensional mathematical operations. SciPy dovetails nicely with NumPy, providing additional capabilities such as optimization, linear algebra, integrals, signal and image processing, amongst others.

Our data analysis toolkit would remain incomplete without acknowledging the power of statistical computing brought forward by packages like statsmodels. It lets us perform a range of statistical tests, model fitting, and statistical data exploration.

As we move further into the realm of advance analytics, Python's machine learning libraries including Scikit-learn, TensorFlow, and Keras take center stage. They offer a plethora of machine learning algorithms to experiment with - from simple linear regression to complex deep learning algorithms.

Once we equip our Excel environment with Python's data-scraping capabilities using libraries like BeautifulSoup and Scrapy, Excel evolves into a dynamic tool fetching real-time data and instantly updating analysis and predictions.

Fairy tales of this tech symbiosis can't be completed without beautiful and intuitive visualizations. Python's popular plotting library, Matplotlib, and the more advanced Seaborn bring vibrant data visualizations to the table. Also, there's Plotly for creating dynamic and interactive plots, taking data visualization to a new level of interactivity and insight.

When it comes to deploying this newfound Python power for Excel users, tools like PyInstaller, cx_Freeze, and Py2exe play a crucial role, allowing the packaging of Python applications into standalone executables thus hiding implementation details.

The ecosystem is also enriched by continuous integration tools like Jenkins, Travis CI, etc., which ensure code quality, reduce the risk of bugs and syntax errors, and maintain the healthy functionality of your Python-Excel applications.

In an environment where data orchestrates the melody of decision-making, and where diverse platforms dance to the rhythm of integrated capabilities, we find ourselves amidst a symphony of synergy. An orchestration where Python and Excel play resonant notes, creating an ecosystem marked by augmentation and amelioration.

The ecosystem of Python and Excel paints a vivid picture of productivity, power, and unprecedented analytical capabilities. Every intricately woven thread of this tapestry of tools adds depth and resilience to the binary ensemble. Each component, be it a Python library or an Excel add-in, plays an essential role in harmonizing the environment, thereby constructing a framework of interconnected powerhouses wherein lies the potential to reform data management and analytics paradigms.

This climactic convergence of Python and Excel's ecosystem brings forth a new era in data analysis - where dynamism meets familiarity, where power meets ease, and where potential meets the tools to harness it. In this grand scheme, we discern an unyielding synergy, a synergy that propels the evolution of data handling, tailoring tomorrow's data landscape.

Inspirational Success Stories

Success is often marked by a trail of resilience; it's a collage of experiences, dotted with victories achieved and obstacles overcome. At the junction of Python and Excel, there spawn triumphant tales that inspire, educate, and motivate. They remind us that when innovation intertwines with determination, great success emerges.

One such account is that of an international retail chain that wanted to overstep traditional data analysis boundaries. Previously, their data driven processes were rooted in the manual export and segregation of reports from their system into Excel for analysis. This approach was time-consuming and offered limited scope for deeper insights.

They made a breakthrough by integrating Python with their Excel workflows. It enabled them to automate the data collection and reporting process, significantly reducing time spent on manual tasks. Crucially, by employing Python libraries such as pandas for data manipulation, and matplotlib for data visualization, they begun to uncover profound insights from their data. They optimized their supply chain, alleviated unnecessary expenditures, improved inventory management, and boosted their customer satisfaction rates. The integration of Python into their Excel environment opened new avenues for business intelligence, driving their growth and market domination.

Another success story comes from a healthcare research center that was grappling with the challenge of managing and analyzing an immense set of patient data. Python made it possible for the center to seamlessly cleanse, manipulate, and ingest this data into Excel sheets for further computation and analysis. Machine learning libraries like scikit-learn and TensorFlow helped them forecast patient responses to different treatment protocols, enhance healthcare delivery, and improve patient outcomes. The combination of Python's analysis capabilities and the readability of Excel dramatically improved the center's research operations, leading to major breakthroughs in their field.

Even beyond businesses and institutions, the fusion of Python and Excel has propelled the careers of individuals. Consider for instance, the tale of an Excel analyst working in a top investment banking firm. Eager to enhance his skills, he decided to step into the world of Python and integrate it with his masterful knowledge of Excel. Leveraging platforms like xlwings and PyXLL, he was able to automate complex financial models, implement advanced data manipulation and analysis techniques, and build comprehensive real-time financial reporting tools. His newfound ability to perform tasks quicker and more accurately, elevated his performance at work, leading to his rapid advancement within the company.

Similarly, let's look at a data scientist who was working with a FinTech startup. Being an adroit Python user, she was skilled in developing sophisticated machine learning algorithms. However, her non-technical team found it difficult to comprehend the insights due to the pythonic complexity. By integrating Python with Excel, she was able to present her complex machine learning algorithms in the familiar lands of Excel. This enabled the organization to make effective, data-driven business decisions quickly, leading to greater success in their endeavours. Consequently, her innovative approach earned her respect and recognition within her organization and even the broader FinTech industry.

Lastly, a remarkable case of a Risk Management Consultant in the banking sector. Predominantly dealing with huge data sets for credit risk calculations and regulatory reporting, the consultant was able to digitize and streamline the entire risk-reporting framework by making use of Python. With the help of libraries such as NumPy, pandas and Openpyxl, he automated data collection from multiple sources, conducted rigorous statistical analysis and validation checks, and exported the results back to reporting templates in Excel. The introduction of robust error-checking and debugging procedures also helped to create a reliable and accurate delivery process that was highly appreciated by the top management.

Tales that Shone Brightly: Python and Excel Breeding Success Stories

Through these chronicles of achievement, we absorb the profound impacts that the union of Python and Excel has on various domains. These stories not only inspire but serve as powerful reminders of the monumental potential that nests within the marriage of these two powerful platforms.

Such success stories bring a sense of purpose and excitement to those sitting on the cusp of their Python-Excel learning journey. These tales, rooted in diverse sectors, assure us that the amalgamation of Python with Excel is not just a mere novelty, but a force that sparks transformation in professional and business landscapes.

In them, we see the reflection of our aspirations, we learn from the triumphs and trials of these pathfinders, and most importantly, we get inspired to carve our own victorious narrative at the confluence of Python and Excel. Through

Python and Excel, we all hold the power to script our inspirational success story.

A Final Project: Your Turn to Shine

We are at the threshold of an exciting opportunity, the inception of a project that will thread together all the knowledge you've gathered about Python and Excel. Pairing aspects of creativity and technicality, it's your chance to embark on this unique journey and let your brilliance radiate.

The final project revolves around creating a dynamic financial dashboard using both Python and Excel, showcasing the versatility and power of their integration. The dashboard will include creating real-time data importing, manipulating the data using Python libraries, generating visualizations, and allowing user interactions. Here are the steps to achieve this:

1. **Data Collection**:

Your first step is to collect data. Considering the objective of creating a financial dashboard, you can select a trading API like Alpha Vantage or EOD Historical Data to fetch your data. Python, with its requests library, can easily pull this data from the API endpoints.

2. **Data Cleaning and Transformation**:

Once the data is acquired, Python's pandas library comes in handy to clean and transform the data. You can handle missing values, convert data types, filter and sort data, and perform various operations to prepare the data for analysis.

3. **Data Analysis**:

After ensuring the data has been correctly cleaned and transformed, you start the analysis part. It involves generating descriptive statistics (like mean, median, standard deviation), rolling averages, correlations, or other relevant financial indicators.

4. **Data Visualization**:

Now that we have clean data and some analysis performed, we would like to present the results in a user-friendly manner. Using Python libraries like matplotlib or seaborn, we can create a multitude of visualizations such as line graphs, histograms, scatter plots, and many more. These visualizations can then be exported into our Excel dashboard.

5. **Integrating with Excel**:

For exporting data back to Excel, we can use the pandas `DataFrame.to_excel()` function. You can create multiple sheets for different views or sets of data within Excel. Through Python's xlwings library, you can even run your Python code within Excel, enabling other users to refresh the dashboard when needed.

6. **Creating Interactive Controls**:

Finally, for making the dashboard interactive, Excel's built-in Form Controls could be used, which include combo boxes, scroll bars, and radio buttons. You can also make use of conditional formatting to highlight certain results, making the dashboard more informative and intuitive to use.

But don't just stop here; extend this project as you see fit. Incorporate elements that align with your interests or requirements. For example, you could add machine learning algorithms through Python when dealing with large datasets, use complex Excel formulae for specific calculations, or even make use of Python's web scraping capabilities to extract additional information.

"You hold the Canvas: Drafting Success with Python and Excel"

This final project serves not just as an evidence of your learning but as a testament to your ability to utilize Python and Excel in unison with striking effectivity. Remember, your victory isn't just in reaching the finish line but also in the journey undertaken, the hurdles abyssed, and lessons learned.

As you embark on this final project, envision it as a stepping stone towards your successful career at the interface of Python and Excel. Hold steadfast the notions of exploration, curiosity, and challenge, and you'll find yourself thriving in an environment rich with potential.

Beyond the pages of this book, lies a world where the harmony of Python and Excel is increasingly celebrated. As we conclude this chapter and you seize the reins of creativity, remember, this isn't an ending, it's only just the beginning. You're about to script your success story; embrace the journey, let your innovation fly, and allow your proficiency in Python and Excel to truly shine.

I look forward to your contributions to the exciting saga that is Python for Excel. Here's to your successful trajectory, and may your voyage illuminate pathways for others setting forth in this realm. Happy coding!

Farewell and Next Steps

The world of Python and Excel is vast, constantly evolving, a dance between the known and the unknown, the explored and yet to be explored. Through this book, you've marked significant progress in mastering these essential tools, but the true journey begins now. Your newly acquired skills bring with it the capacity to extend, expand, and continue learning, adapting to the dynamic flux of the field.

1. Keep Exploring

With the foundational code structures and advanced methodologies of Python and Excel solidly in your toolkit now, an ocean of exploration awaits. Consider engaging with other libraries of Python that weren't covered in this book. For instance, Django (a Python web framework) can lead you into the realms of web development, while Pygame can offer insights into game development with Python. Simultaneously, continue to hone your Excel skills, mastering functionalities like Power Query, Power Pivot, and Power Maps.

2. Dive into Open Source

Open-source projects provide a fantastic space to employ and magnify your skills. Participating in these projects allows you to contribute to the community while simultaneously improving your own abilities. Platforms like GitHub offer a host of Python and Excel projects, where you can contribute and learn from global professionals.

3. Tap into Community Resources

Forums like Stack Overflow, Reddit, and numerous blogs and tutorials online are all vital cogs in your journey of continual learning. Make use of these platforms to pose queries, share knowledge, and consistently evolve. Engage with the Python and Excel communities, share your projects, ask questions, and maintain your growth trajectory.

4. Stay Abreast of Upcoming Trends

The tech realm is ever-evolving, with advancements succeeding each other in rapid succession. Keep abreast of the latest developments, trends, and dynamic shifts of Python, Excel, and their overlapping functionalities. Subscribe to relevant newsletters, follow thought leaders and influencers on social platforms, and stay in tune with latest releases and updates.

5. Continue Building

Put your skills to active use by working continuously on real-life projects. Whether it's a workplace assignment or a personal project for honing your skills, continuous practice is the fastest pathway to mastery. Your final project, the financial dashboard, is a solid stepping-stone. Utilize it as an inspiration to conceive, design, and realize even more complex and intricate projects in the future.

Remember that the boundaries of where your learning stops are defined only by yourself. In realities of programming and spreadsheet wingmanship, the beauty is in their limitless possibilities. With Python and Excel as your formidable accomplices, you are more than equipped to stride confidently on this path of endless potential.

In the grand scheme of things, this book has been just a speck of the knowledge universe, albeit a significant one, that has empowered you with the ability to manipulate and comprehend data in a new light. As we part ways at this juncture, remember that your journey doesn't cease here. This book has merely sown the seeds of knowledge, and it's now unto you to nurture, grow and evolve these nascent learnings into a thriving forest of expertise.

From enhancing present company systems to contributing to open-source projects or devising revolutionary applications, you're commencing onto a future that promises unbounded potential and exponential growth. As you pave the roads to untapped opportunities and unrivaled triumphs, may every obstacle revive your vigor, every challenge grow your resilience, and every achievement catalyze your thirst for learning.

You're not just a programmer or an Excel expert anymore, but a craftsman who molds these tools to infuse efficiency, accuracy, and effectiveness into data analysis and manipulation. As we draft the conclusion to this fascinating narrative of Python and Excel, we can't wait to witness the countless success stories that you are about to pen. Best wishes on your quest, and may the pixels ever be in your favor.